Theory of the Firm

C. J. HAWKINS

Lecturer in Economics
University of Southampton

Macmillan

First published 1973 by
THE MACMILLAN PRESS LTD
London and Basingstoke
Associated companies in New York Dublin
Melbourne Johannesburg and Madras

SBN 333 12016 7

Printed in Great Britain by
THE ANCHOR PRESS LTD
Tiptree, Essex

The rapid growth of academic literature in the field of economics has posed serious problems for both students and teachers of the subject. The latter find it difficult to keep pace with more than a few areas of their subject, so that an inevitable trend towards specialism emerges. The student quickly loses perspective as the maze of theories and models grows and the discipline accommodates an increasing amount of quantitative techniques.

'Macmillan Studies in Economics' is a new series which sets out to provide the student with short, reasonably critical surveys of the developments within the various specialist areas of theoretical and applied economics. At the same time, the studies aim to form an integrated series so that, seen as a whole, they supply a balanced overview of the subject of economics. The emphasis in each study is upon recent work, but each topic will generally be placed in a historical context so that the reader may see the logical development of thought through time. Selected bibliographies are provided to guide readers to more extensive works. Each study aims at a brief treatment of the salient problems in order to avoid clouding the issues in detailed argument. None the less, the texts are largely self-contained, and presume only that the student has some knowledge of elementary micro-economics and macro-economics.

Mathematical exposition has been adopted only where necessary. Some recent developments in economics are not readily comprehensible without some mathematics and statistics, and quantitative approaches also serve to shorten what would otherwise be lengthy and involved arguments. Where authors have found it necessary to introduce mathematical techniques, these techniques have been kept to a minimum. The emphasis is upon the economics, and not upon the quantitative methods. Later studies in the series will provide analyses of the links between quantitative methods, in particular econometrics, and economic analysis.

MACMILLAN STUDIES IN ECONOMICS

General Editors: D. C. ROWAN and G. R. FISHER

Executive Editor: D. W. PEARCE

Published

John Burton: WAGE INFLATION
Miles Fleming: MONETARY THEORY
C. J. Hawkins: THEORY OF THE FIRM
C. J. Hawkins and D. W. Pearce: CAPITAL INVESTMENT APPRAISAL
David F. Heathfield: PRODUCTION FUNCTIONS
Dudley Jackson: POVERTY
P. N. Junankar: INVESTMENT: THEORIES AND EVIDENCE
J. E. King: LABOUR ECONOMICS
J. A. Kregel: THE THEORY OF ECONOMIC GROWTH
D. W. Pearce: COST-BENEFIT ANALYSIS
Maurice Peston: PUBLIC GOODS AND THE PUBLIC SECTOR
David Robertson: INTERNATIONAL TRADE POLICY
Charles K. Rowley: ANTITRUST AND ECONOMIC EFFICIENCY
C. H. Sharp: TRANSPORT ECONOMICS
G. K. Shaw: FISCAL POLICY
R. Shone: THE PURE THEORY OF INTERNATIONAL TRADE
Frank J. B. Stilwell: REGIONAL ECONOMIC POLICY
John Vaizey: THE ECONOMICS OF EDUCATION
Peter A. Victor: ECONOMICS OF POLLUTION
Grahame Walshe: INTERNATIONAL MONETARY REFORM

Forthcoming

G. Denton: ECONOMICS OF INDICATIVE PLANNING
N. Gibson: MONETARY POLICY
Richard Lecomber: ECONOMIC GROWTH AND ENVIRONMENTAL QUALITY
George McKenzie: THE MONETARY THEORY OF INTERNATIONAL TRADE
D. Mayston: THE POSSIBILITY OF SOCIAL CHOICE
B. Morgan: MONETARISM AND KEYNESIANISM
S. K. Nath: A PERSPECTIVE OF WELFARE ECONOMICS
A. Peaker: BRITISH ECONOMIC GROWTH SINCE 1945
F. Pennance: HOUSING ECONOMICS
N. Rav: TRADE CYCLES – THEORY AND PRACTICE
M. Stabler: AGRICULTURAL ECONOMICS
E. Roy Weintraub: GENERAL EQUILIBRIUM THEORY
J. Wiseman: PRICING PROBLEMS OF THE NATIONALISED INDUSTRIES

Contents

Acknowledgements   6

1   Introduction   7

2   Neo-Classical Theories of Profit Maximisation:
    Origins   11

3   Profit-Maximisation Models: Specific Criticism   17
    The perfectly competitive model   17
    Pure monopoly   22
    Monopolistic competition   23
    Oligopoly and duopoly   27

4   Developments of Profit-Maximisation Models   31
    Price leadership models   31
    Dominant firm price leadership   32
    Barometric price leadership   34
    Collusive price leadership   34
    Price leadership and interdependence   35
    The kinked demand curve model   36
    Entry forestalling   38
    Costs of production   44
    X-inefficiency   50
    Long-run profit maximisation   51
    Uncertainty   54
    Game theory   56

5   Alternative Models to Profit Maximisation   60
    Utility maximisation   62
    Sales revenue maximisation   64
    Output maximisation   68
    Constrained output and profit maximisation   69
    Behavioural theories   70
    Cost-plus pricing   73
    Growth models   77

6   Conclusion   81

References   85

Acknowledgements

'The' theory of the firm now consists of so many different approaches that no summary of this length could possibly encompass all of them. What I have tried to do is to pull together major developments which have had a continuing impact. Such a selection is inevitably personal, but references have been selected which are not just important in their own right but which, via their own bibliographies, lead the reader to other interesting works. If emphasis on traditional theory is not very great, it is because the aim has been to supplement standard micro-economics textbooks.

I should like to thank Professors Pearce, Rowan and Wise of Southampton University for valued comments on earlier drafts, and Maurice Townsend, also of Southampton, for many detailed corrections. I should also like to thank Mary Mundye for her patient typing and retyping of successive drafts. And in particular I should like to thank David Pearce, without whose editorial pressure the book, like the subject, could have been a never-ending pursuit.

C. J. H.

1 Introduction

The theory of the firm is one of the cardinal elements of economics because of the variety of uses it serves throughout the whole of economic analysis. Nothing could be more short-sighted than to dismiss it as an isolated, slightly esoteric area of micro-economics with very little practical application, as theory for theory's sake. On the contrary, knowledge of the way in which firms behave is essential in almost every field of economics because firms are decisively involved in the determination of such major variables as investment, prices, employment, output and wages. From the applied macro-economist trying to solve the problem of inflation, to the most abstract of growth theorists devising optimum growth paths over a time-horizon of infinity, almost everybody involved in economics will be using some results derived from the theory of the firm when constructing their models.

Unfortunately the theory of the firm is currently in a state of considerable confusion. Many economists are disillusioned with profit-maximisation models but are not yet able to agree on a generally acceptable alternative theory.

All intuition suggests utility maximisation as the 'right' alternative to profit maximisation, if only because it is tantamount to being a tautology – to saying that firms do what they want to do. None the less, we have used this kind of tautology elsewhere in economics and to good effect: maximum utility is the goal often attributed to consumers, wage-earners and society as a whole. It would provide a pleasing symmetry to our subject if we could use it for firms as well. Why then is it not used?

The reluctance of most economists to pursue utility-maximising models for firms is due to the knowledge that so many factors (e.g. profit, sales, output, growth, number of staff and expenditure on plush offices and cars) are likely to give utility to people in industry that we shall end up with a model incapable of yielding any definite results. The results of a tax on labour, for example, could be either an increase or a decrease in the number of people employed, depending on the precise form of the firm's utility function.

This is the overriding problem for the theory of the firm. We need realistic models of how firms really do behave, and at the same time we are expected to provide definite results for the other areas of economics.

Not surprisingly, this need for precise and definite results has led economists – though in dwindling numbers – to cling to the traditional tool-kit in the absence of a replacement of equal simplicity. A theorist interested in general equilibrium analysis would naturally prefer, other things being equal, to be told 'Firms pay a real wage to labour equal to the value of the marginal physical product' (a standard result of the perfect competition model) rather than to be told 'The wage paid by firms will vary with the strength of their preference for staff numbers as against profits' (which would be the result of a utility-maximising model where some decision-makers were assumed to enjoy 'empire-building').

There is therefore a dilemma. On the one hand we have the profit-maximising model which yields precise, readily applicable results; on the other is a seemingly endless array of theories, individually persuasive but often mutually contradictory. Yet it is surely part of the excitement of this sector of economics that it is passing through a period of ferment from which new formulations of knowledge will emerge.

In the history of any subject there will be times when the standard accepted theories which yielded effective results in the past are increasingly seen to be no longer capable of explaining the realities of the present. In the days when capitalists came in one kind and two sizes (small and very small), it may have been plausible for Adam Smith to say that the entrepreneur 'intends only his own gain, and he is in this, as in many other cases, led by an invisible hand to promote an end which was no part of his intention'. As a result, he thought that in general the allocation of resources would be 'as nearly as possible in the proportion which is most agreeable to the interest of the whole society' [1]. Economic analysis still shows that a welfare optimum, of a kind, can result from firms pursuing their own profits, provided there is a sufficient number of small firms. None the less, it would be doing Adam Smith an injustice to imagine that he would not have wanted to think again when confronted with I.C.I. and General Motors.

Nor is it simply the emergence of industrial giants that makes this an epoch of change, but also the dramatic way in which the old style of capitalist/entrepreneur has been split into shareholders who own and managers who manage.

Given such far-reaching changes in the character of 'firms', it is hardly surprising that we should be in the throes of change in our theorising about them. Nevertheless, until an effective replacement can be offered for the established neo-classical theory, it must still be central to any discussion of the theory of the firm. We begin therefore with an examination of the traditional theories and an outline of the major developments that have been made from them (Chapters 2 to 4). Subsequently, in Chapter 5, the principal alternative theories to profit maximisation will be discussed.

Most of these modern theories have sprung from the observation that profit in traditional theory is far too narrow a motive. So instead they have typically analysed the effects of firms getting utility from some other *particular* factor, such as output, sales or growth. If, as now seems inevitable, the theory of the firm moves progressively towards the assumption that firms get utility from *many* factors (rather than just one or two), then it may well be that all these theories will find some place as part of a utility-maximising approach. In short, we may find that the theory of the firm will become an amalgam of existing theories and no doubt of some new ones as well.

Inevitably, the resulting theory cannot be so simple and easily handled a tool as the traditional one, nor as capable of yielding the sweeping generalisations that are often needed to provide 'definite results', but it should eventually be far better suited to the wide range of modern industry.

2 Neo-Classical Theories of Profit Maximisation: Origins

Almost the whole of today's standard profit-maximisation theory of the firm is derived from the neo-classical models developed during the early part of this century. The models of Alfred Marshall [7], Joan Robinson [11] and Edward Chamberlin [12] are still taught, not as relics of the past or mere pedagogical devices, but as integral parts of the basic structure of modern economics. While their role in the future development of our subject is increasingly being questioned, no one can doubt their importance in bringing us to where we are today.

The origins of the theory of the firm naturally go back way beyond Alfred Marshall. Men have pondered for centuries the causes of market value and the age-old paradox that seemingly useless diamonds command a higher price than an essential like water.

The first attempt to put together a theory of prices in anything like a modern economic form was by Adam Smith in 1776 [1]. In particular, Smith was concerned to find the 'right' or 'natural' price of goods – that 'central price to which the prices of all commodities are continually gravitating'. He thought the answer to value lay in a good's cost of production. Market value might deviate from costs of production on a day-to-day basis, but eventually prices would fall to the good's 'natural' value – its production cost.

In primitive societies, labour would be the sole cost of production and the best unit for measuring value: 'If among a nation of hunters, for example, it usually costs twice the labour to kill a beaver which it does to kill a deer, one beaver should naturally exchange for or be worth two deer.' But he realised – if reluctantly – that his labour theory of value applied only to 'that early and rude state of society which precedes both the accumulation of stock and the appropriation of land'. As societies developed and accumulated capital and as land fell into private hands, Smith saw profit and rent as necessary parts of cost. Later, in 1803, Jean-Baptiste Say [2] added entrepreneurship as the fourth of the basic factors of production still used by many economists to this day. And by the end of the classical period John Stuart Mill [3] had made more explicit the nature of production costs when he wrote:

> If one of two things commands, on the average, the greater value than the other, the cause must be that it requires for its production either a greater quantity of labour, or a kind of labour permanently paid at a higher rate; or a capital, or a part of the capital, which supports that labour must be advanced for a longer period; or lastly, that the production is attended with some circumstance which requires to be compensated by a permanently higher rate of profit ([3] p. 480).

Classical economists' concern with cost of production and natural values did not lead them to ignore market prices altogether: these were seen as being determined by supply and demand, but marked differences between the market and the natural price were looked on as temporary deviations. The emphasis on costs of production as the prime determinant of value came about because from Adam Smith to Mill the classicist believed that in the long run the forces of competition would, in the absence of monopoly, cause natural and market prices to coincide. And it is worth recalling that this conclusion is still consistent with modern perfectly competitive models which reach equilibrium where long-run average cost equals price. The idea that changes in the level of output would alter production costs and hence prices based on them did not begin to be fully explored until the beginning of this century.

But before that, the cost-of-production approach to value came under fire from a growing belief in the utility approach.

Rather curiously, although the basis of diminishing marginal utility had been discussed by Jeremy Bentham as early as 1780 [4], marginalism and the utility approach to value, which together led to the development of the demand side of the theory of the firm, did not get fully under way until the 1870s. It was then that the pioneer marginalists began to emerge simultaneously in several parts of Europe. Some entirely discarded the classical cost-of-production theory of value and, like Carl Menger [5] in Vienna, thought that 'whether a diamond was found accidentally or was obtained from a diamond pit with the employment of a thousand days of labour is completely irrelevant for its value'. Utility was the prime determinant of value.

At the same time, Stanley Jevons in England said he had come 'to the somewhat novel opinion that *value depends entirely upon utility*' [6]. Diamonds being dearer than water, although of far less use, was only a paradox if we thought only of total utility. Certainly, we would rather have all water and no diamonds instead of the other way round. But we would rather have *more* diamonds than more water. It was not diamonds' total utility but their higher marginal utility that caused their higher value. Despite his rejection of costs of production and, in particular, of labour theories of value, he at times conceded them an *indirect* effect on value in that by affecting supply they caused utility to vary. None the less, utility was given the primary role: the value of labour 'must be determined by the value of the produce, not the value of the produce by that of the labour'.

Alfred Marshall, in England, whose *Principles of Economics* was published in 1890 [7], was also refining and developing the utility approach to demand. But unlike the mainstream marginalists, his major contemporaries, he saw no real conflict between the utility and cost-of-production approaches to value. To Marshall, and to succeeding neo-classical economists, the natural value of a good was its market price determined by the forces of supply and demand: neither supply (based on costs of production) nor demand (based on utility) could be regarded as the pre-eminent factor in the pricing process. As Marshall put it: 'We might as reasonably dispute whether it is the upper or the under blade of a pair of scissors that cuts a piece of paper, as whether value is governed by utility or cost of production' ([7] p. 348).

But Marshall did much more than resolve the value dispute. He developed the demand side of the theory of the firm considerably beyond the work of his forebears and rooted it firmly in utility theory. He specified demand as a schedule of price/quantity relationships with all other prices held constant – the strict partial approach.[1] And he saw clearly the existence of parameters which could induce the demand curve to shift. Elasticity of demand, fixed and variable costs, the distinction between the short and the long run in micro-theory and between internal and external economies of scale, are all areas where he made major contributions, building the basis of the profit-maximising theories in use today.

Monopoly was looked on by Marshall as a rarity, as a deviation from the norm, so that the world could best be typified by competition. In some industries rising production costs would limit the growth of firms. In others, despite the existence of economies of scale of which he was aware, he did not think firms would in general reach monopoly status because 'in almost every trade there is a constant rise and fall of large businesses, at any one moment some firms being in the ascending phase and others in the descending. For in times of average prosperity decay in one direction is sure to be more than balanced by growth in another' ([7] pp. 315–17).

Firms would eventually decline despite economies of scale

[1] This standard micro-economic technique, although enabling us to isolate the effect of each variable, one at a time, has been much criticised. Cournot [8] for one, although he used the technique extensively, was worried about the effect of changing one price on the demand for other products. Although he foresaw the need for general equilibrium analysis, he thought it 'would surpass the power of mathematical analysis and of our practical methods of calculation'. By the 1870s, however, Léon Walras [9] had shown general equilibrium analysis to be possible, albeit under highly restrictive assumptions.

because the original owner and driving force would die and pass the business 'into the hands of people with less energy and less creative genius, if not with less active interest in its prosperity'. So industries could be approximated, he thought, by competition and by using the costs of a representative firm which was neither the most nor the least efficient.

Marshall's decline-and-fall-of-firms theory found little long-term favour, and elsewhere the emphasis moved to rising costs as the factor limiting the growth of firms.

A curious feature of early neo-classical economics is that it developed almost nothing to fill the chasm between the extremes of competition and monopoly. There were various duopoly models dating back to Cournot [8], but these were regarded as special cases of monopoly. The predominant belief of early neo-classical economists was that either competition or monopoly could be used to approximate most real-world situations. And as a result it was possible to concentrate on analysis of the *industry* rather than the firm. If there were many firms in an industry, it was assumed they had no influence on price; if there was one or very few firms, control over price would be near enough that of a pure monopolist.

A major breakthrough occurred in 1926 when Sraffa [10] put forward the view that even if there were many firms competing against each other, they could none the less influence price: there could be competition without horizontal demand curves – and there could be downward-sloping demand curves without monopoly.

The importance of this innovation was that it offered an alternative to the then widely held view that it was rising production costs (due to diseconomies of scale) that prevented firms expanding output without limit. Sraffa disputed this explanation, arguing instead that 'the majority of those which produce manufactured consumers' goods work under conditions of individual diminishing costs'. If they could sell all the output they liked at a given price, they would expand enormously. But in practice, to sell more they must reduce price. And reducing price would not gain them the whole market because of different consumers' preferences for different brands.

15

Although the economies-of-scale argument had already been emphasised by Marshall, and even earlier by Mill, Sraffa's novel suggestion that there could be many firms in an industry that was highly competitive, and yet each could have influence on price, caused intensive rethinking of the theory of the firm and led eventually to the modern emphasis on brand loyalties, advertising and product differentiation. Out of the rethinking in England came in 1933 Joan Robinson's *The Economics of Imperfect Competition* [11], while independently in America Edward Chamberlin's *The Theory of Monopolistic Competition* [12] was published in the same year (Robinson's work was based directly on Sraffa's article, while Chamberlin's was a development of his own dissertation written in 1927).

To this day, virtually the whole of the standard profit-maximising theory of the firm is derived from and based upon the Chamberlin–Robinson models. They were among the pioneer users of the marginal approach to the theory of the firm – an approach which gave the well-known single law for all firms, from pure competition to pure monopoly, that if profits are to be maximised, marginal cost and marginal revenue must be equated.[1]

[1] Cournot [8] had used differential calculus in 1830 to derive marginal cost and marginal revenue and the need for their equality if profits were to be maximised. But curiously his work had little impact. And since Marshall analysed firms without these concepts (although he was one of the few who had read Cournot), economics had to wait for their rediscovery until the 1920s – almost a century after Cournot had first used them. For the origins of marginal cost and revenue, see Shackle [13].

3 Profit-Maximisation Models: Specific Criticism

Ever since Sraffa made the opening move, perfect competition has been the most harangued of the traditional models. But the others have been criticised too, and in the process the nature of the conditions facing firms in the spectrum of market situations from competition to monopoly has been clarified.

This chapter looks at some of the problems which are linked specifically to particular models. Discontent has been widespread not just with the specific models, but also with the general assumptions underlying the neo-classical approach. Profit maximisation as a firm's only motive is just one example of an assumption which has been savaged from many different directions. These more general problems, and the developments that have taken place to meet them, form the basis of Chapters 4 and 5.

THE PERFECTLY COMPETITIVE MODEL

In terms of the mileage of economic literature to which it has led, perfect competition must surely rate as the most important of all the models of a firm; in terms of its relevance to reality in its *strictest textbook forms*, it must surely rate as the least. Rarely has such a mountain of theory been erected on such a pinhead of empirical fact. But unfortunately we are faced here, *par excellence*, with the choice between realism and theoretical results. It can be argued that crude models of perfect competition approximate to the production of certain products; but crude models do not yield precise mathematical results. By contrast, if we refine the model sufficiently we arrive at the most beautifully symmetrical results imaginable: almost every important variable turns out to be definitely and precisely equal to almost every other – marginal cost equals average cost which in turn equals marginal revenue which is itself equal to average revenue. It is the precision and simplicity of these results which makes perfect competition so easy to incorporate and manipulate in the models used in other areas of economics. But many have questioned whether the assumptions necessary to achieve these results are often, or ever, met fully in practice.

For example, most manufactured products, far from being homogeneous, are branded, differentiated and advertised; it is perhaps natural therefore in developed Western economies to be rather scathing about the perfectly competitive model and to claim that it is relevant only in the case of organised exchanges which exist for securities and some commodities. But there are two things wrong with this near-total rejection of the model. One is that, although the strict assumptions of the model are rarely if ever *fully* met, neo-classicists never intended their models to be an exact fit for any particular set of conditions; they merely intended them to be a good enough fit to enable predictions to be made about firms' behaviour in general. And certain industries have been argued to *approximate* to the perfectly competitive model (see Hendry [14]; Reynolds [15]). Secondly, it should be borne in mind that the great bulk of the world's agricultural output is produced under conditions not so very far different from those of the competitive model. No one, for example, could argue that the small farmers of Nigeria could individually have any effect on the world market price for groundnuts. Their behaviour may not exactly fit the model, but it may be explained by it, at least in general terms. It must be admitted, however, that the perfectly competitive model is nowadays of little relevance to manufacturing industry; nor can we be too stringent in applying its assumptions even to much of agriculture where, although its

18

general predictions are of value, it has yet to be shown that we can realistically assume that the *precise* equilibrium results will generally (or ever) be attained. It may be fair to assume that there is a tendency towards the equilibrium, but this does not mean that we can assume that the equilibrium results always hold. In other words, even if we find an economy where all the major sectors approximated to perfect competition, it still would not mean that at any point in time we could say that all producers were exactly at the point where marginal cost equalled price. They might merely be striving in a complex world to get as near to that point as they could. Similarly in physics, the effect of gravity, *ceteris paribus*, may be correctly isolated by showing that a feather will fall at the same speed as a piece of lead in a perfect vacuum; but before predicting the results of dropping objects off London Bridge, some modifications must be made for the complexities of reality.

The major criticism of perfect competition, therefore, has centred round the difficulty of finding markets to which it applies in anything more than a very approximate way. In particular, the assumptions that all firms produce identical products,[1] and that there are so many firms that none can individually affect price, have led to its being of trivial value in industrial economies. It does, however, provide a useful model for looking at agricultural production on a fairly general level, provided the need to meet the precise textbook assumptions is not pressed too rigorously.

Perfect competition is normally treated as a static model, but its dynamics have been examined and cobweb models have been developed. The basis of these is, for example, that demand may be a function of today's price while supply may be a function of yesterday's price. Since consumers and producers are responding to different pieces of information, there is no reason why supply and demand should match in any period.

---

[1] Strict homogeneity of product is not necessary. For example, farmers may produce milk of different fat content, but provided the prices they get systematically reflect fat content in a way directly related to production costs, then the homogeneity assumption is not infringed. Transport costs can be treated in a similar way.

Hence, as in Fig. 1, a cobweb pattern may emerge. Firms supply Q_1 on the first day and the price they get is P_1. This leads them to supply Q_2 on the second day which yields a lower price P_2. So they reduce supply to Q_3 and the price goes up to P_3, and so on. Fig. 1 shows a process which will converge to where the two curves cross. But supply and demand curves of different slope can lead to a divergent or even to an oscillatory

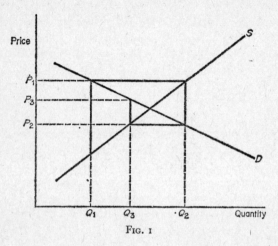

FIG. I

process. For an assessment of cobweb models see Akerman [16], and for an appraisal of their use to explain commodity price cycles see Ezekiel [17].

Much criticism has arisen over the traditional view that perfect competition is better from the social point of view than other forms of competition. Schumpeter [18] has attacked the static nature of the model and has argued that some freedom from competition, and some extra profitability, must exist to encourage firms to bear the costs and take the risks of research and development to generate growth and to develop new products and new technologies. Chamberlin [12] attacked the idea that a world of homogeneous products is really what most of us want. Monopolistic competition may give a less efficient allocation of resources, but it offers in exchange a great variety of differentiated products which one may prefer. We

20

may prefer to pay more not to all drive the same type of car and have the same style of shirt. He argued that 'The explicit recognition that product is differentiated brings into the open the problem of variety and makes it clear that *pure competition may no longer be regarded as in any sense an "ideal" for purposes of welfare economics*' ([12] p. 214).

Chamberlin goes on to argue that in welfare economics, as well as the ideal prices and outputs, we need to add the problem of selecting ideal differentiations of product and ideal selling expenditures.

J. M. Clark ([19], [20]) argued even more forcefully that perfect competition 'does not and cannot exist and has presumably never existed' [20], and that it is not therefore a valid ideal with which to compare the real world. It is, he argued, quite meaningless as a result of economies of scale to compare the Ford Motor Company, worldwide, with competition and to ask which is best. Demand for Ford cars would need to be astronomic to allow an indefinitely large number of firms to produce them at an economic level of output. This level of demand does not exist in reality and neither does the alternative, which is a production process which would be economic at tiny levels of output. There is little point, he concludes, in comparing reality with something which does not and could not exist. What is needed, Clark argues, is some idea of a workable form of competition – an 'ideal' that could exist in practice, a standard of comparison relevant to the world we live in. His seminal work led to a rash of papers (ably surveyed by Sosnick [21]) which have put forward many interesting ideas, but which have not yet, unfortunately, led to general agreement on a basis for 'workable competition'.

Other aspects of perfect competition which have been questioned relate mainly to assumptions which are also used for the other neo-classical models, and these will be discussed in Chapter 4 below. For a survey of the development of economic thought on perfect competition see Stigler [22]; for discussions of the welfare aspects of the model see Graaff [23] and Little [24]; and for an interesting essay on the inadequacy of perfect competition as a 'real-world' model see Samuelson [36].

PURE MONOPOLY

There is no dispute about the analytical content of the pure monopoly model. Given the static context, no competitors' reactions to worry about, the absence of potential new entrants to fend off, and a desire to maximise profits, we can say little more than that the firm should pursue all activities to the point where the marginal cost of the activity equals the marginal revenue it produces. This rule applies equally to production, advertising, packaging, research and every other variable which the firm can control.

Models have been developed to show the effect of a monopolist discriminating between buyers in different markets and of a monopoly seller being faced by a monopoly buyer (a 'monopsonist'). Examples can be found in any basic micro-economics text. But these are extensions of the 'monopoly' model rather than developments of it.

Some disenchantment with the model has occurred because of the difficulty of accurately defining 'pure' monopoly in a way that still allows us to find plausible real-world examples. In some sense, everything competes with everything else. A monopoly producer of gas must still compete with electricity, coal and oil. I.C.I. had a patent on 'Terylene' but still had to compete with nylon and rayon, with cotton and wool. A national airline must still compete with foreign airlines, at least on overseas routes. It must also compete with road and rail in the home market. For this reason, many economists feel that although some industries at first sight seem to fit the pure monopoly mould, they are usually better analysed using oligopoly models. Even nationalised industries, which often come close to the pure monopoly form, are scarcely realistic examples of the model since they are rarely asked to maximise profits.

None the less, the monopoly model is a useful part of the economist's tool-kit and it does define and illustrate one extreme form of behaviour. And we should not look only for industrial juggernauts dominating a national market in order to find monopoly. If the nearest pub is ten miles away, the local landlord may exhibit many of the symptoms of the pure monopoly model.

MONOPOLISTIC COMPETITION

Chamberlin [12] assumed a large group of firms producing differentiated products. They were faced by downward-sloping demand curves which were not kinked. Using U-shaped cost curves and assuming free entry and exit, he derived the equilibrium depicted in Fig. 2. The Robinson model is essentially similar. dd' shows the firm's demand curve if none of its competitors follows any price change; DD' shows demand if all firms charge the same price. Chamberlin assumed firms would always expect dd' to be relevant (since they are a tiny part of the market and the effect of their actions on others is taken as trivial). But in practice, since all are given the same cost and revenue functions, they all change price together and move along DD'.

The long-run equilibrium in Fig. 2 is achieved by (a) the

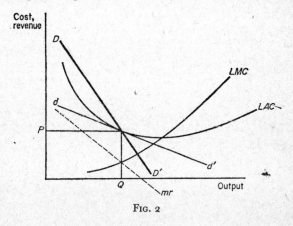

FIG. 2

dd' curve shifting down the DD' curve as prices are cut, and (b) the DD' curve shifting down and to the left as new firms enter the industry reducing potential sales for existing firms. Since firms believe dd' is relevant and not DD', they have no

23

incentive to disturb the equilibrium which is at the now familiar tangency position between dd' and the long-run average cost curve.

Product differentiation and selling expenditure are treated in essentially similar ways to the pricing decision: the most profitable level of each will be selected in conjunction with the most profitable price, and in equilibrium new entrants will have eroded all supernormal profits.

One of the major problems with this model centres round the difficulty of defining the group of firms who are in monopolistic competition. Stigler [25] has argued that the group could 'include all of the firms in the economy'. This follows, he says, because 'taking any one product as our point of departure, each substitute has in turn its substitutes, so that the adjacent cross-elasticities may not diminish, and even increase, as we move farther away from the "base" firm in some technological or geographical sense'.

Although the interrelationships between all the products available in a modern industrial society are undoubtedly complex, many would argue that it is generally possible to draw boundaries around groups of firms producing fairly similar products such that there is in some sense more competition between firms within the boundary than with those outside it. Although motoring must compete with railways and the whole broad spectrum of different means of transportation, there is no doubt that Fords are more affected by British Leyland's prices than they are by the prices of an imported Japanese moped.

None the less, there has been a protracted dispute about the problem of defining the group and about the conditions necessary to achieve demand curves of the type which Chamberlin specified (see Triffin [26], Bishop [27], [28], Chamberlin [29], Fellner [30], Heiser [31]). In particular, it has been shown (see Bain [32]) that, under certain conditions, Chamberlin's dd' curve could approach infinite elasticity as the number of firms increased. This would occur if each firm's cross-elasticity with the other firms in the group (E_{ji}) did not decrease at least proportionately with the increase in the number of firms (n). Each firm's own-price elasticity (E_{ii}) would then inevitably get larger as the number of extrants increased. This follows from Chamberlin's assumptions that all firms have the same price and output and that every product in the group has the same degree of substitutability for all other products in the group (i.e. that all E_{ji}'s are equal).

Therefore, $E_{ii} = E_{ji} (n-1)$. And the greater the number of firms, the more elastic will dd' be, unless E_{ji} decreases at least proportionately with the increase in the number of firms. Chamberlin [29] asserts that it will, but no one has yet shown that this must necessarily be so. Therefore, dd' may become horizontal and the price/output equilibrium may be the same as for perfect competition. Monopolistic competition would still be different from perfect competition, however, because of product differentiation and selling expenditure.

Nicols [33], in an important article, has shown that Chamberlin's assumption of downward-sloping demand curves with no kinks can hold only under restrictive conditions about the scales of preference of all the different buyers for the products of all the firms in the group.

Since firms are faced by a downward-sloping demand curve in Chamberlin's model, his tangency solution inevitably occurs to the left of minimum average cost in Fig. 1. This has led to the comment that monopolistic competition leads to excess capacity and to production at higher than minimum cost.

Many have criticised this implication of the model, arguing that the entrepreneurs are assumed to ignore the fact that maximising short-run profits leads to new entrants reducing the size of their market. Various models based on the concept of entry forestalling have been developed (see Chapter 4).

One way and another – in fact in almost every way – Chamberlin's monopolistic competition model has been pounded and battered with relentless ferocity. That it has survived – albeit much weakened in generality – is because whatever one may feel about Chamberlin's particular assumptions and his particular development of them, he none the less tackled, and led others to tackle, an important and real problem. There can be little doubt that the types of market conditions that Chamberlin and Robinson analysed are prevalent in practice. After all, we do see hosts of petrol stations, shops, hotels and pubs, all of which can (and some do) charge different prices without gaining or losing all the market. And we do see far more of these than is consistent with all working at full capacity: none is faced by a market price from which it dare not deviate for fear of selling nothing at all. If economics has not done much with the model that Sraffa led it to, then one could argue that that is the fault of economists and not of the model. The model, after all, offers far more scope than do the simple and rather clinical competition and pure monopoly models. Variations in quality, packaging, servicing, advertising, delivery, guarantees and so on are all features which were introduced as essential parts of the decision-making process in firms. Their introduction has made the subject more complex; it has also made it potentially far more realistic.

Certainly, the model needs modifying and developing. The symmetry assumption (that all cross-elasticities are equal), for example, seems to be neither a generally realistic nor a necessary feature of the model. Equally, the uniformity assumption – that all firms have the same cost and revenue curves – can be scrapped, as Bain [34] has suggested. Different firms may produce different qualities or variations of the product with inevitably different costs. Hence firms may be of different size, have different prices and produce different (though similar) products all within the same market. Provided there is free entry for new firms, profits will still be eroded and each firm can have an equilibrium similar to that in Fig. 2.

It may be objected that when the assumption of complete uniformity of firms is dropped, and especially if entry is not entirely free, then firms may be very different from each other. And making simple unambiguous statements about them may be difficult or even impossible, as Stigler has argued [25]. Similarly, empirical testing of propositions may be impossible with the kind of data that is usually assumed or readily available, as Archibald has pointed out [35]. But if the world

26

really is as complex as Chamberlin has suggested, then these are less criticisms of the model than complaints about the complexity of reality. For an excellent range of assessments of the impact of monopolistic competition on economic theory, see Kuenne [36], and for a rather 'anti-Chamberlin' view see Telser [37].

OLIGOPOLY AND DUOPOLY

The basic duopoly model used in economics was developed by Cournot in 1838 [8]. He found determinate solutions for price and output. But he needed strict assumptions about firms' behaviour to do this. He assumed that firm A would make a conjecture about how its rival would vary output in response to any move that A might make. In particular, he assumed that this *conjectural variation* would be zero, i.e. that each firm decided what level of output to produce on the assumption that its rivals would not vary their output.[1]

If we have data on each firm's production costs and on their demand curves, we can quite simply derive, say, firm B's profit-maximising responses to any output set by firm A (*given the assumption that A will not change output whatever move B makes*). Given this assumption, we can plot firm B's optimum responses to all possible output levels which A could set. This gives us B's *reaction function*. We can get A's reaction function in exactly the same way; these are depicted in Fig. 3.

Suppose firm A begins by producing output a_1. Firm B believes that A will hold this output constant whatever B does. On this assumption, it pays B to move to output b_1 (on his reaction function); so he does so. Firm A then moves to output a_2 (shown by his reaction function) and B responds by moving to b_2. The process continues until equilibrium is reached where the reaction functions cross at X. If, however, we reverse the slopes (so that A has B's reaction function), then the firms will move away from point X and not towards it. Much

---

[1] The model can be equally well manipulated by assuming firms adjust prices instead of output.

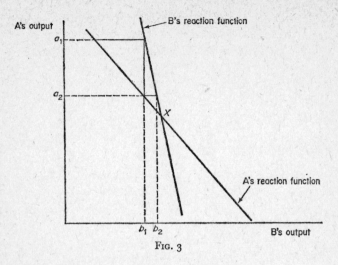

FIG. 3

depends on the slope of the functions, and if we make the model dynamic, the timing of responses is important as well.

The basic Cournot model has been widely criticised. Every time firm A makes a move he assumes B will not respond. Yet B always does: he always changes output. Even if this has happened a hundred times with monotonous regularity, A assumes it will not happen next time. Meanwhile B makes the same assumption about A's behaviour, however formidable the evidence he has received to the contrary. Not to put too fine a point on it, the model works only if the firms are run by mental defectives.

A major step forward in oligopoly theory was made when Chamberlin [12] asserted that oligopolists with even rudimentary intelligence would recognise their interdependence: 'If each seeks his maximum profit position rationally and intelligently, he will realise that when there are only two or a few sellers his own move has a considerable effect upon his competitors, and that this makes it idle to suppose that they will accept without retaliation the losses he forces upon them.'

He went on to argue that once the joint profit-maximising price has been reached, no firm will reduce price since it recognises that the others will respond and all will be worse

28

off. He concluded that 'although the sellers are entirely independent, the equilibrium result is the same as though there were a monopolistic agreement between them'. But Chamberlin's conclusion, that all would choose the joint profit-maximising price, holds only if all firms in the industry have identical cost and revenue functions. If different firms face different production costs (owing to differences in location, technology, age of plant or efficiency) or have different demand curves (owing to brand images, advertising, product differentiation and the like), then it is clearly possible for firms to want different prices. A price war may result. Or, if the firms make very similar products so that in the long run none dares charge a higher price than the others, the one wanting the lowest price can set it knowing the others must eventually follow.

Alternatively, the firms may decide to collude and charge the joint profit-maximising price; but in this case, where cost or revenue conditions differ, one or more firms may be worse off at the joint maximum than if they had operated independently and set the price that maximised their own profits. The other firms may need to bribe them to compensate for the loss of profits: output-sharing agreements may be used to achieve the same effect. Monopoly investigations have shown that the conclusions we derive from these simple oligopoly models occur frequently in practice.

An alternative approach to the oligopoly problem is the Stackelberg leader–follower model [38]. This may be outlined as follows. Firm A can choose to be a leader (A then assumes that B will treat A's output as given), or A can be a follower (in which case he assumes B's output is given and works out his best move on that basis). If A and B both choose to be follower, the basic Cournot solution is reached since each firm treats the other's output as given, as they do in Cournot's model. If A leads and B follows, there is also a determinate stable solution. But if both firms choose to lead, then there will not be a stable equilibrium until one or other firm gives in and becomes a follower.

A vast range of duopoly and oligopoly models can be

29

developed by specifying particular assumptions about each firm's behaviour. Every possible motivation can be attributed to the firms in the model. And each may give a different solution. For example, we could assume that one firm aims at a fixed share of the market: if the other firm allows it to get its desired share, there is a stable equilibrium; it it does not, there isn't.

The enormous number of possible models has led many to despair of our ever finding generally applicable determinate solutions to the oligopoly problem. The answer, if there is one, depends entirely on what each firm guesses the others will do – and in turn on what they guess the first firm will do. In response to this feeling that there are an endless number of possible ways for firms to behave, many economists have felt that, instead of hypothesising further and expanding the traditional models outlined above, it would be better to develop new models based on evidence about actual behaviour. These new models are outlined in Chapter 4. A further major advance has been the development of 'game theory' (see pp. 56–9), which provides useful insights when applied to the oligopoly problem.

4 Developments of Profit-Maximisation Models

A number of major developments have been made to the theory of profit-maximising firms in order to meet the fairly intense criticism of the early models and also to bring them more into line with empirical evidence. There has also, of course, been intensive activity on the technical level, extracting more and more detailed results from the basic models – results which now form the major part of any modern micro-economic textbook (see Baumol [39], Hadar [40], Horowitz [41]). Important though these technical efforts have been, they have contributed largely an extension of our knowledge of the implications of the basic model. And that, of course, is what they were intended to do. But there have also been developments which have significantly altered the basic models so as to change radically our predictions about the way in which profit-maximising firms will behave. It is to discussing a number of the more important of these radical developments that the rest of this chapter is devoted.

PRICE LEADERSHIP MODELS

A number of models have been developed to meet evidence that some markets seem to be best typified by the assumption that one firm acts as the price leader, who sets the price, while the other firms merely follow suit. Price leadership may arise because one firm is much larger than the rest (dominant firm price leadership), but it may also arise if one firm is conventionally first to make price changes which are typically followed by the rest of the firms in the industry (barometric price leadership). And the third major leadership model assumes that the other firms tacitly collude with the leader in order to maximise joint profits.

DOMINANT FIRM PRICE LEADERSHIP

In this model the largest firm is assumed to estimate what sales all the other firms in the industry would make at various possible prices: by deducting the other firms' sales from its estimate of the industry demand curve, the dominant firm can arrive at its own estimated demand curve. Given a knowledge of how its costs of production respond to changes in output, the firm can then select the price which maximises its own profits. The dominant firm's position may be based either on the fact that it can produce more output than the other firms at any given price (owing to lower production costs) or to the fact that consumers demand more of its product than they do of the products of the other firms. Either way, the model represents an industry with one large firm and a number of smaller ones.

An example of dominant firm price leadership is given in Fig. 4, where DD' is the industry demand curve, and SS' is the small firms' supply curve. If the market price is OB (where SS' cuts DD'), the small firms would be prepared to meet all available demand. So this is the price at which the dominant firm's demand curve cuts the vertical axis. At a price of OS the small firms will supply nothing, so the dominant firm's demand curve becomes CD' (the industry demand curve) at prices below OS – and outputs above OE. Intermediate points on the dominant firm's demand curve are derived in the following way. At a price OA the small firms will supply AF. Industry demand will be AI. By deducting a distance $HI=AF$ from industry demand, the dominant firm can find that an amount AH of its product will be demanded at the price OA. In this way the dominant firm can derive its demand curve BCD'.

32

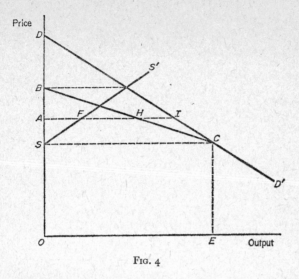

FIG. 4

It can then add the marginal revenue and marginal cost curves in the normal way to derive its profit-maximising price/output levels.

Considerable empirical evidence exists on dominant firm price leadership (see, for example, Colberg *et al.* [42] and Kaplan *et al.* [43]).

Although the dominant firm's problem is simplicity itself in the static model, long-run considerations may make reality far more complex. In particular, the dominant firm will have to look at the effects of its short-run policy on the long-run output of its rivals, and on the possibility of encouraging new entrants. As an example, if long-run production costs are constant and equal for all firms, then the dominant firm can stop the small firms growing and new firms entering the industry only if it sets a price which allows it to make no profits above normal. But it could do better than this by setting a higher price, making profits in the short run and accepting a long-run decline in its market share (see Worcester [44]). There is empirical evidence of firms behaving in this way (see Markham [45], Hession [46], Stigler [47]). For the problem of forestalling new entrants see pp. 38–44 below.

BAROMETRIC PRICE LEADERSHIP

Barometric price leadership does not involve the price leader in being the dominant or largest firm in an industry. A small firm may be accepted as typically the first one to make price changes. Provided it consistently changes price to levels that the other firms find acceptable, there is no reason why its price leadership should not continue despite its not being the dominant firm in the industry. Stigler [48] gives an example where the price leader produced less than one-seventh of the industry total output – and this price leader was eventually succeeded by an even smaller firm. In short, in this model the price leader can be regarded as acting merely as the barometer of feelings of other firms, or at least of making changes sufficiently near to those desired by other firms for them to feel it not to be worthwhile stepping out of line. One of the major problems with the barometric leadership models is the difficulty of distinguishing examples of it from those of collusive price leadership (see Markham [49] and Kaplan *et al.* [43]).

COLLUSIVE PRICE LEADERSHIP

Markham [49] specified the conditions for collusive price leadership as being an industry where, firstly, firms recognise that they are better off 'co-operating' in pricing policy than in going their separate ways and, secondly, where there is a considerable amount of discretion possible in the choice of price (e.g. no very close substitutes for the industry's products). The implication of this situation is that price will tend towards joint profit maximisation.

The important point is that the firms are not formally colluding to fix the price that jointly makes them best off. They are following a price leader because they believe his prices are near enough to what is best for them all and because they believe that doing this is better than risking a policy of going it alone. Collusive price leadership may, for example, come about after painful experiences in a price war. The problem for the price leader is to choose a price which the others will accept. It can do this by compromising between the conflicting interests of different firms (if they have different cost structures). Or it may impose its own preferred price – especially if it is the lowest-cost producer. But the problem is easiest and the model most relevant when firms face similar cost and revenue conditions. For an example of collusive price leadership see Tennant [50]; for a general discussion of the merits of leadership models see Bain [51] and Lanzillotti [52]; for a comment on Markham's views see Oxenfeldt [53]; and for a wide-ranging discussion and development of the problems of firms in oligopoly see Fellner [54].

Collusive price leaders have the same long-run problems as dominant firms. If they set the short-run joint profit-maximising price that suits the major firms in the industry, production may be so profitable that smaller firms (if they exist in the industry) will expand production and pursue larger shares of the market. Equally, new firms may enter the industry. But if there are economies of scale – or other important barriers to entry – the major firms may be able to make reasonable profits and retain a major share of the market even in the long run, provided they do not set prices to maximise short-run profits but instead choose a price low enough to make production relatively unprofitable for new and small firms (see pp. 38–44 below).

If, instead of following a price leader, oligopolists decide to collude formally, there are problems of enforcing the agreement and of detecting secret price cuts by competitors. For an interesting model which incorporates these problems see Stigler [55].

PRICE LEADERSHIP AND INTERDEPENDENCE

The ease with which determinate solutions can be derived from price leadership models is due to the simple nature of the other firms' reactions – they merely follow the leader's price change. We therefore have no need of complex procedures for each to guess the other's reactions. The fact that these leadership models are well supported by empirical evidence may suggest that firms accept a price leader simply because this provides a practical means of solving the complexities which have been shown to be involved in the oligopoly problem. Perhaps some men prefer to take the easy way out even if it is sometimes less optimal than solving a problem the hard way. Or perhaps even our complex models underrate the true complexity of the problem. Perhaps firms learn from experience that price wars benefit none of them – at least in industries where fixed costs are high. Each can match the other's price cuts in the short run since it pays no one to cease production even if prices are cut below full cost, so long as variable costs are covered. Only if price is kept below full cost until existing plant and machinery become obsolete or fall apart does it pay anyone to leave the industry. And that may take ten years or more. Since the discounted value of profits ten years hence is low compared with profits in the near future, the net present value of the price-war policy is not likely to be very attractive. So firms may learn that, in capital-intensive industries at least, policies of 'live and let live' make a good deal of sense. Accepting a price leader is perhaps the most obvious and simplest of 'live and let live' policies. But some barrier to entry such as economies of scale must protect the major firms and at the same time the leader must not be too greedy in the short run or the high profits will encourage new entrants. The industry will then become more and more competitive and there will be too many firms for leadership to work.

THE KINKED DEMAND CURVE MODEL

In 1939 Hall and Hitch in Britain [56] and Sweezy in America [57] published almost simultaneously their views that oligopoly markets might best be represented by models using kinked rather than conventional demand curves. The basis of the argument is that if an oligopolist cuts price, the other firms will

36

follow suit rather than face a significant drop in sales. On the other hand, if one firm raises price the rest will not follow but will prefer to watch it suffer a dramatic decline in sales. As a result of this asymmetric response to price changes, the demand curve will be kinked at the ruling market price, i.e. the demand curve will be relatively elastic for price increases but relatively inelastic for price decreases, as in Fig. 5 where P_0 is the current market price.

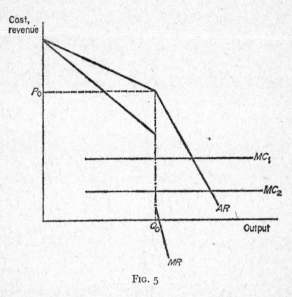

FIG. 5

The kink in the demand curve at the current market price leads to there being a discontinuous section in the marginal revenue curve. In Fig. 5 profits are maximised at an output of Q_0 where the marginal cost curve cuts the discontinuous section of the marginal revenue curve. The normal argument is that considerable shifts in demand may occur, and/or considerable changes in costs of production, while still leaving the marginal cost curve passing through the discontinuous section in the marginal revenue curve: as a result, in the case of demand shifts the optimum output will change but the profit-maximising price will remain unchanged, and in the

37

case of shifts in production costs, e.g. from MC_1 to MC_2 in Fig. 5, neither the optimum selling price nor the optimum output will have altered.

The model has been used, therefore, as a possible explanation for price rigidity in oligopolistic markets. Empirical evidence, notably that of Stigler [48] and Simon [58], has not, however, given much support to the price rigidity conclusion. Recently, too, this argument has been questioned on theoretical grounds and the model has been extended to cover price leadership(see Pashigian [59], and Hawkins [60]). None the less, the kinked demand curve has been a major development in the theory of the firm, has found itself a place in most modern textbooks, and can be plausibly argued to be a useful weapon in the economist's armour for analysing and explaining the behaviour of firms.

ENTRY FORESTALLING

Early criticisms of the implication that the Chamberlin monopolistic competition model led to excess capacity in equilibrium eventually brought forth entry-forestalling models of the modern type. Harrod in particular [61] argued that instead of setting a short-run profit-maximising price, firms would set a price that yielded only normal profits and so discourage new entrants. Such a policy, however, will yield a zero net present value if discounted at the 'normal' cost of capital. Entry forestalling to make economic sense requires 'barriers to entry', i.e. factors such as economies of scale, established brand images and the like which make it possible for existing firms to make higher profits than new entrants can expect to make. Once there are barriers to entry, existing firms can set a price which allows new firms to make only normal profits (which should discourage entry) but which allows the existing firms to make supernormal profit. Entry forestalling can then yield a positive net present value.

The problem for entry-forestalling models is in part at least to decide whether it pays to forestall entry (and make fairly low profits for a long time but with a big market share) or instead to go for short-run maximisation in the Chamberlin way (making high early profits, but accepting a reduced market share and excess capacity in the long run owing to pressure from new entrants).

There is by now an enormous literature on the subject (see [61]–[79]) which has gradually extended the model to fit oligopoly as well as monopolistic competition. Among the most important of the pioneer attempts to incorporate entry forestalling into models of firms' behaviour were those of Andrews

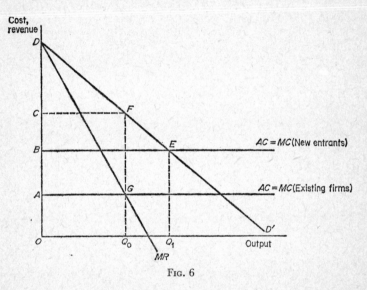

FIG. 6

[62], developed by Edwards ([63], [64]), and of Bain in America [65][1]. Bain is also responsible for the classic work on barriers to entry [66], an essential feature of all models.

To make life easy, the simplest model assumes that DD' in Fig. 6 is the long-run industry demand curve which is assumed

---

[1] A much earlier development of the basic case for entry forestalling was made by Kaldor in his article, 'Market Imperfection and Excess Capacity', *Economic Journal* (1935). This is one of many examples of ideas in economics being developed, forgotten, and then redeveloped later. Cournot's development of marginal revenue is another example.

to be static through time. Average costs for existing firms are constant at OA and, being constant, are equal to marginal costs. New entrants' average costs are higher at a level OB owing to barriers to entry.

What is the existing firms' long-run demand curve? DD' is static and conventionally would be thought to fit the bill. But if existing firms use prices above OB (the new entrants' AC) new firms will enter the industry, and if price is held above OB new entrants will keep flooding in until demand for existing firms' output approaches zero. One can therefore argue (as Clark [19], Harrod [61] and Andrews [62] have done) that, in the long run, prices above OB are irrelevant since they cannot be sustained: the long-run demand curve therefore becomes virtually infinitely elastic at the price OB. Prices below OB can of course be set and yield positive sales even in the long run. The existing firms' demand curve in the long run is therefore BED' (if they forestall new entrants).

If, however, the existing firms maximise profits in the conventional way, they will use DD' as their demand curve and equate MC and MR at a price of OC and output of OQ_0. Industry profits will be $ACFG$ per period. New entrants will then be attracted. The total demand for existing firms' products will fall, i.e. their share of total industry demand will fall so that for them a new demand curve below and to the left of DD' will be relevant when new firms enter. If they use this new demand curve to maximise profits in the conventional way – instead of truncating it at the entry-forestalling price to give a horizontal section like BE – then new firms will continue to enter and demand for existing firms' output will continue to fall; and it will go on falling until the 'limit' price, OB, is reached, at which point entry will cease.

It should be noted that owing to barriers to entry there will be supernormal profits for existing firms even in the long run (equal to $OB - OA$ per unit of output). The question firms need to answer is, does it pay to extract high short-run profits (like $ACFG$) and end up with low long-run profits (of AB per unit) *on the small level of output made necessary by new entrants taking more and more of total industry demand*? Or does it pay to set straight

40

away the entry-forestalling price OB and make for ever a profit of AB per unit *on the larger entry-forestalling output of* OQ_1?

The answer, of course, depends on how fast new firms are expected to enter the industry while high short-run profits are being made. The faster they are likely to enter, and the more of them that are expected, the more it pays to set an entry-forestalling price. The answer also depends on the extent of the barriers to entry and the rate at which firms discount future profits.

Four main cases exist:

(a) Where there are no entry barriers so that the 'limit' price equals long-run average cost (including normal profits). In this situation there is no incentive to forestall entry. It pays to make short-run supernormal profits while you can. This is termed the 'easy entry' case.

(b) Where there are entry barriers but the cost advantage of existing firms is not enough to make it worthwhile forgoing short-run profits in order to forestall new entrants. This is the 'ineffectively impeded entry' case.

(c) Where entry barriers are big enough to make entry forestalling pay. This is the 'effectively impeded entry' case.

(d) Where barriers to entry are so large and therefore existing firms' cost advantage is so great that the limit price is higher than the short-run profit-maximisation price. This case – 'blockaded entry' – enables existing firms to take short-run profits and be free from the threat of entry. They can maximise profits in the conventional short-run way.

In cases (a), (b) and (d) conventional short-run profit maximisation pays, while in (c) long-run profits are maximised by setting a limit price.

The entry-forestalling policy has important implications for theory. The conventional marginal analysis no longer holds, though it does pay the firm to operate where the marginal curve to the long-run 'demand curve', BED', equals marginal

41

cost. But note that this is not the same as the marginal revenue curve to the conventional demand curve DD'. (This unconventional MR curve will have a discontinuous section below E, owing to the kink in BED'.) What is most interesting is that it pays the firm to set price on a cost-plus basis using a mark-up which is not quite big enough to attract entrants. If costs increase, price can be raised (because the entry-forestalling price will increase too). Firms need not worry about elasticity of demand or marginalism: they need only set the limit price and sell all they can.[1] Unexpected demand shifts can be catered for by stock changes, not price changes. In this way, full cost-plus pricing without marginalism or any sophisticated techniques becomes the optimal long-run policy for maximising profits.

An appealing feature of the entry-forestalling model is that it is capable of considerable development. For example, a model of Bain's has been developed by Sylos-Labini [67] (and further developed by Modigliani [68]) to show that entry forestalling can pay even if new firms can produce at costs similar to those of existing firms.

Put simply, the reason is that when there are considerable economies of scale, new entrants must make large outputs in order to be economic. Their entry will therefore cause significant excess capacity. Bain and Sylos-Labini have suggested that existing firms may respond to new entrants by holding output constant. So the market price must fall after entry. It follows that existing firms can hold price above production costs by an amount equal to the drop in price which new entrants expect to be caused by their additional output. The calculation of this surplus of pre-entry price over costs depends critically on the assumption that existing firms will hold output constant after entry has taken place. But of course, other reactions are possible, and we can rapidly get back to all firms guessing what each other's responses will be in the usual oligopoly model way. It is, however, 'irrational' for existing firms to hold output constant. It does not make them the most profit. It may well

[1] The problem is more complex if AC curves are U-shaped and the firm operates where marginal costs are rising.

pay them not to hold output constant. But in any case these problems only arise because we are trying to see how high the entry-forestalling price can be: they do not destroy the concept. There is surely always one price which existing firms can set to forestall entry[1] – and that is a price which would not enable new firms to make more than normal profits whatever level of output they chose.

A further development of the limit-pricing model is to drop the assumption that firms must adopt one or other of the two extreme policies (either high short-run profits or limit pricing). In practice, it may pay to shade price gradually over time down to the limit price and accept a trickle of new entrants but not encourage a deluge. Selecting the optimum pattern of prices over time is a complex problem involving the calculus of variations. In practice, firms no doubt use judgement, but, given adequate data (or rather forecasts of future values), the problem is soluble mathematically ([69]–[72]). A further complexity is that instead of choosing between *certain* entry and no entry, firms may set price to reduce the *possibility* of entry (see Kamien and Schwartz [73], [74] and Williamson [75]). And if we drop the assumption of static industry demand, one might even argue as Bhagwati does [76] – that in a growth market *current* prices cannot deter new entrants since they will be attracted by *future* prices resulting from *future* growth. It is difficult to see how existing firms could indicate convincingly to new entrants what their future pattern of prices was going to be.

It is difficult to verify empirically the prevalence of entry forestalling, especially since the rate of return earned in different industries may be affected by many factors other than just the height of the barriers to entry. Bain, however [77], has derived some interesting preliminary evidence which has been followed up and confirmed by Mann [78]. What the evidence shows is that firms in highly concentrated industries (where the concentration ratio for the top eight firms exceeds 70 per cent) made markedly higher rates of return than firms in less concentrated industries. The evidence also shows that in these

[1] i.e. in the static model.

highly concentrated industries rates of return were typically highest where barriers to entry were 'very high'. But it was not possible to show that rates of return were substantially different where barriers were 'substantial' rather than 'moderate to low'. As Mann admits, 'the limit price hypothesis, then, remains neither confirmed nor rejected'.

Using an alternative approach, based on estimates of elasticity of demand, Wenders [79] has shown that pricing policy for U.S. automobiles appears consistent with limit pricing but not with conventional short-run maximisation of profits. And Comanor and Wilson [80] have presented some impressive evidence on the role of advertising as a barrier to entry.

The possibility of forestalling new entrants was a major omission from traditional theory and is now widely regarded as one of the most important new developments in the theory of the firm.

COSTS OF PRODUCTION

There has been a long-drawn-out, and as yet still unresolved, dispute among economists as to the behaviour of firms' costs of production, especially in the long run. Traditionally, the long-run average cost curve of a firm is assumed to be U-shaped: the initial fall is assumed to reflect economies of scale which continue until output is raised to an optimum plant size; thereafter diseconomies of scale are assumed to set in. Traditionally, it has been argued that as the firm gets larger it will experience diseconomies in management, administration and selling. Even the most modern micro-economic textbooks tend still to be based on predominantly U-shaped long-run average cost curves, despite the fact that there is mounting empirical evidence to suggest that costs of production do not generally rise as firms expand, i.e. to suggest that long-run average cost curves are L-shaped – either flat or falling as in Fig. 7. For evidence, further references and discussion of the problems of measurement, see Wiles [81], Johnston [82], Pratten [83],

Pratten *et al.* [84] and the N.B.E.R. price studies ([85] and [86]). For examples of the more sceptical viewpoint see Smith [87], Friedman [88] and Silbertson [89].

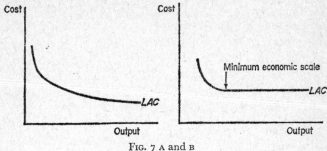

FIG. 7 A and B

It is surprising that even today an economist may feel mildly heretical in suggesting that an L rather than a U best describes the behaviour of long-run costs of production of firms. It is surprising because even before the beginning of this century John Stuart Mill had noted that 'there is a tendency to substitute more and more, in one branch of industry after another, large establishments for small ones' [3]. And Marshall, despite his belief that the economy could generally be represented by a competitive structure, none the less saw the possibility that the production of certain commodities might conform 'to the law of increasing returns in such a way as to give a very great advantage to large producers' [7].

Economists today are still divided over the importance of economies of scale. At one extreme there are those who believe that L-shaped long-run average cost curves are rarely if ever relevant; at the other are those who believe that they are typical at least of modern manufacturing industry.

P. J. D. Wiles has argued strongly for the adoption of L-shaped cost curves as the norm [81]. After reviewing a considerable amount of empirical evidence, he concludes that

the long-run average cost curve descends like the left-hand branch of a capital U, swiftly at first and then more gently. Decreasing costs with size are almost universal. But the U

45

seldom turns up again. *Sharply increasing costs with size are practically unknown, and even slight increases are rare.* Sixty per cent of the examples obey what we may call the *law of L-shaped costs*. Another 31 per cent show a slight increase of costs in the largest size-class. Most but by no means all of these slight increases are well within the expected margin of error that any empirical correlation should show.

Johnston, in what is now a classic work [82], summarises and reviews a wide range of empirical studies and provides an excellent 'critique of the critics'. For him, the impression which stands out most clearly is 'the preponderance of the L-shaped pattern of long-run average cost that emerges so frequently from the various long-run analyses'.

Most recently, the Department of Applied Economics at Cambridge has completed what is probably the most extensive analysis so far of industry-by-industry data on the behaviour of costs of production in Britain (see Pratten [83], and Pratten, Dean and Silbertson [84]). Surveying the final data of twenty-five major industries, Pratten concludes: '. . . our estimates show that there are substantial technical economies of scale for the production of many products.' But in addition to economies on the production side, it was also found that large firms 'can achieve economies by spreading certain marketing and management costs, and in some cases by spreading expenditure on research'. The Cambridge study is not encouraging for any who may feel that economies of scale are a temporary problem; it concludes that both the magnitude of economies of scale, and the range of output to which they apply, are increasing over time. It should be noted, however, that as with all empirical testing the results are open to interpretation, and Silbertson [89] argues that the Cambridge study shows relatively few industries still experiencing significant scale economies when output is related to the size of the U.K. market.

Opponents of L-shaped long-run average costs curves base their case either on criticisms of the technical validity of much of the empirical evidence (criticisms which are in certain cases well founded), but more especially on the belief that, even though empirical evidence overwhelmingly suggests constant or falling average costs up to levels of output so far experienced, there must none the less come a point, as output is increased, when diseconomies of scale will eventually make themselves felt. Arguments about what may or may not happen in the far distant future at hypothetical output levels are unfortunately impossible to refute with evidence about what is happening now. One way out of this dilemma is to say that, in so far as economics is concerned with predicting what will happen to our economies in the *near future*, we should accept that for many products L-shaped long-run average cost curves best fit the available empirical evidence; and we should go on doing so until such time as empirical evidence begins to lend weight to the theoretical arguments for diseconomies of scale.

Economics which deals with longer time-horizons has a more difficult problem. None of us knows what the effects of prolonged growth (if it happens) and new technologies will be. Ideally, we should look at every possibility and compare the results, i.e. we should not exclude the possibility that long-run cost curves may all become U-shaped, or all L-shaped, or there may always be a mixture of both.

The effect of incorporating L- rather than U-shaped average cost curves in the theory of the firm is significant. Perfect competition is seen to be impossible: a horizontal demand curve combined with a flat or falling cost curve gives an explosive situation with no equilibrium output. It is always profitable to expand output and eventually the firm must reach the situation in which it can affect the market price. Once this situation has been reached and the firm is faced by a downward-sloping demand curve, we can select the usual equilibrium where marginal cost equals marginal revenue. Outside perfect competition, one might be tempted therefore to conclude that L-shaped cost curves do not make very much difference; the equilibrium for each firm is the same. But the significant point is that in those industries where economies of scale extend out to very large levels of output (a falling L-shaped cost curve as in Fig. 7A), the number of firms in the

47

industry will become very small, ultimately perhaps being reduced to only one.

Even in those industries where average costs become constant, there may still be very few firms if, for example, the minimum economic scale of output (see Fig. 7B) is large relative to the total market. L-shaped cost curves lead us, therefore, to expect higher concentration levels than do the U-shaped curves of traditional theory. This expectation is, incidentally, supported by empirical evidence on industrial concentration in Britain, America and elsewhere (see, for example, Utton [90]).

Despite controversy about the prevalence of L-shaped long-run average cost curves, there is little doubt that they exist in *some* industries at least up to the levels of output which we have so far achieved. And accepting the possibility of L-shaped long-run cost curves, at least for some industries, is an important modification of traditional theory.

For discussion of the implications for the theory of the firm, and for economics as a whole, of long-run economies of scale, see, for example, Clark [20], Samuelson [36], Kaldor [91], and Wiles [81]. And for the welfare effects of economies of scale on the problem of mergers and monopoly, see Williamson [92] and Rowley [93].

As for the behaviour of production costs in the short run, empirical evidence has suggested nothing more startling than that the short-run average cost curve is skewed rather than symmetrical. Average costs, it seems, tend to a minimum when plant is working at or near designed maximum output. Beyond designed capacity, costs rise almost vertically. Some writers have argued that no firm would operate on the almost vertical dotted section in Fig. 8, and so the short-run average cost curve should therefore be described as L-shaped falling all the way to designed maximum output. In fairness, however, there seems to be no good reason why one should not include the information that if one attempts to raise output past the designed maximum, it is virtually impossible to do so except at the expense of a very dramatic increase in costs. After all, it is the knowledge that costs behave in this way that prevents

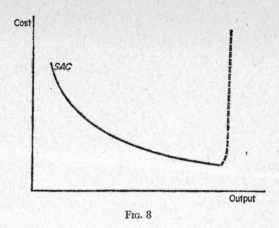

Fig. 8

most firms from operating on the near-vertical section. If this information is included, then we achieve the skewed U-shape in Fig. 8.

The incorporation of a skewed rather than a symmetrical U-shaped short-run average cost curve in the theory of the firm presents no particular problems and does not lead to any very significant change in our conclusions. The equality of marginal cost (whatever its shape) and marginal revenue is still a necessary condition for maximising profits.

From the applied point of view, the main implication of the short-run evidence is that firms are likely to be highly concerned with achieving full-capacity working so as to minimise production costs – hence the well-known argument of industrialists that a buoyant home market is the best basis for export success. Also implied is the well-known phenomenon that after a period of recession (and therefore excess capacity) it is usually found that production costs fall (or stay fairly steady) during the first phase of expansion.

It should be noted, though, that micro-economic cost curves assume constant factor prices (as well as constant technology). A change in these parameters will cause the cost curves to shift. So if wages rise during expansion this will at least partly offset the *ceteris paribus* fall in production costs as we approach full-capacity working.

49

Micro-cost curves show only the cost of producing various levels of output in the most economic way conceivable with today's technology. They show, in short, the very best that is possible if firms are 100 per cent efficient, 100 per cent of the time.

The naïvity of this assumption has led recently to the development of the concept of 'X-inefficiency'.

X-INEFFICIENCY

The basis of Leibenstein's concept of X-inefficiency [94] is that human beings are unlike other factors of production. Machines have a potential output which can be achieved by pressing the right switches. Human beings by contrast can adjust the quality and pace of their work in line with their own preferences. By supervision, by punishments and incentives, human effort can be varied. There is no reason why a shop-floor worker, or a manager, should have a utility function which coincides with that of the firm as a whole or of its shareholders. Employees may be compelled to produce a minimum output – or lose their job. There may also be a maximum output of which they are capable given all the right sticks and carrots. But between these levels they can choose to vary the amount of time they spend on various activities, the pace at which they work and the quality of the work they do. There is no single-valued relationship between the number of man-hours purchased and the quality or quantity of effort that is expended in production. As a result, it is unlikely that every employee's choices will be exercised in such a way as to give maximum output per unit of input. So X-inefficiency almost always exists.

In Leibenstein's view, the production possibility frontier does not exist. There are many frontiers depending on degrees of human effort and so on. But we may wish to choose some plausible maximum conceivable frontier for output and measure the extent of X-inefficiency in relation to that.

Many economists feel X-inefficiency to be more likely the

50

greater a firm's monopoly power – the more it is isolated from competition. Management may consume part of the potential profits in a variety of ways, e.g. by tolerating inefficiency, by overstaffing, and by spending on prestige buildings and equipment. They may also make less effort than they could to keep technologically up to date, scrap old plant, research new products, develop export markets and the like. The more comfortable the situation, the less may be the effort which is expended to improve it.

Empirical testing has revealed considerable evidence of X-inefficiency (Leibenstein [94], Williamson [95], Caves *et al.* [96]). Rowley [93] provides a detailed bibliography and broad survey of developments based on the X-inefficiency concept.

LONG-RUN PROFIT MAXIMISATION

Quite one of the biggest headaches for economists is the realisation that if profit-maximisers are rational they will maximise long-run profits and not short-run profits as neo-classical models assumed. Once this is accepted – and there is now little dissent – profit maximisation becomes a formidable problem.

The firm needs to know (or estimate) its demand and cost functions for every time-period throughout the product's life-span. Ignoring uncertainty for the time being, the firm must then pick that collection of prices through time which will maximise the net present value of its profits. The problem is greatly simplified if the price charged today has no effect on demand in future periods, for then, obviously, it does no harm (and in fact is best) to maximise short-run profits in the conventional way. But suppose, as seems plausible, that a high price today will inhibit the build-up of sales in future, will lose the company goodwill and will let competitors get more entrenched in the market, then maximising short-run profits may harm long-run prospects.

It may seem tempting to use the long-run demand curve and long-run cost curve and derive the optimum from these. But

51

there may be no such thing as a two-dimensional long-run demand curve (see Clark [97]). With price on one axis and output on the other, we are saying, for example, that 100 units will be sold at 50p in the long run. But what does this mean? Will 100 units be sold in every time-period – constant sales for ever and constant price? Or will we have *average* sales of 100 units, in which case this is scarcely relevant to the problem of selecting price in any one period? What is needed is three dimensions, as a first step, with time on the third axis so we can show the price/quantity relationship *in each period*. But even this is not enough. If today's price affects future demand there will be a different set of future demand curves for each possible price today. Nor is that all. There will be yet another different set of future demand curves for each price we could charge tomorrow, and the next day, and the next onwards throughout the project's life. The problem is indeed formidable. No doubt different demand functions for each period could be specified related to all possible past collections of prices, and the problem – probably via complex mathematical techniques – would be capable of solution at least in theory. But no one can believe that firms are indulging in such complicated wizardry in practice, nor that they have – or perhaps ever will have – the data necessary to solve the problem. And aside from demand, firms would need data on all future prices of all inputs in order to derive future production costs. Strictly, they should also know the future effects of all demand parameters such as advertising and packaging, and should know these effects for all possible changes in the product for all future periods.

A number of attempts have been made to find solutions to the problem by simplifying it. The very act of simplification is, however, necessarily suspect, since it may radically alter the conclusions (see, for example, Winter and Phelps [98] and Ball [99]). Both these approaches make the problem manageable by simplifying the demand side of the problem. For example, Ball assumes that competitors' prices are given and do not change, and that industry demand is unaffected by a particular firm's price. He then derives a 'dynamic demand function' which shows that the lower the firm's price the higher will its growth of demand be. Although the model is interesting, the use of a single price and single growth rate through time is an abstraction which limits its scope.

The position of long-run profit maximisation is regrettably that we do not yet have a simple answer unless future demand is unaffected by present prices. Nor is it only a problem of high short-run prices allowing existing competitors to build up a bigger long-run share of the market. There is the problem of how short-run prices affect the number of new entrants and also how they affect the rate at which substitute products are developed if we allow Schumpeter's view that potential competition is mainly from new products rather than from other firms making the same product [18].

None the less, there are several factors which can make the problem at least approachable. Firstly, there is no reason to believe that people running firms are on average as *technically equipped* to solve the theoretical problem as economists are. If we cannot solve it formally and churn out optimum values for every time-period, the chances are they cannot either. So we need to find out what firms actually do when faced with this problem. Evidence suggests they fall back on rule-of-thumb pricing methods. They take present costs, for example, and use their judgement to add on a margin for profit which makes some allowance for the problems of encouraging new entrants, fostering long-run growth of demand and like problems. Economics may want to develop rigorous formal solutions to help firms solve the problem better; but there is no evidence that we need these just to explain and mirror what is happening in reality. In so far as we want to predict, we should perhaps be more concerned with how others solve the problem than with trying to solve it ourselves.

A second helpful approach is to look at the individual factors involved in the long-run problem, like entry forestalling, and see how firms might expect to be affected by these.

Thirdly, the effect of today's price on long-run demand is clearly important if one firm can charge a different price from the others. But if firms typically keep their prices roughly in line with each other, allowing for the costs of producing differentiated products, then the long-run problem is markedly reduced. And if a firm's long-run demand is increased by charging less than its rivals charge, it is unlikely that the rivals will allow price differences to persist. This may in part account for firms in oligopoly at least tending to keep prices in line and pursuing 'live and let live' policies (or even forming price agreements if they can get away with it). Under these conditions, and if long-run *industry* demand is not affected (or not much affected) by short-run *industry* prices, then, as we have seen, the best long-run strategy is to maximise profits in each short-run period – aside from the problem for existing firms of forestalling new entrants.

For a stimulating and wide-ranging discussion of the long-run problems of firms, see Penrose [100].

UNCERTAINTY

As we have seen, firms' decisions involve making forecasts about the future. The neo-classical models got round this problem by assuming all firms had perfect knowledge – not just of their own cost and revenue functions for all future periods, but also those of all the other firms with which they had to compete. Each firm was assumed to know with certainty that all the other firms were profit-maximisers like themselves. In reality, firms will rarely, if ever, be so fortunate as to have anything like so much knowledge as this about the conditions under which they are operating. Joan Robinson, for example, looking back on her own pioneering contribution to neo-classical theory, felt that the assumptions were 'by no means a suitable basis for an analysis of the problems of prices, production and distribution which present themselves in reality' [101]. The data available to firms would be, she thought, 'necessarily extremely vague since the consequences of a given policy cannot be isolated in an ever changing market'. As a result, she thought that 'in reality, evidently, an individual demand curve (for a particular product produced by a particular firm) is a mere smudge, to which it is vain to attribute elegant geometrical properties'.

It is now widely accepted that in practice firms will be certain about very few things. They may have fairly detailed knowledge of their own costs of production, but *certain* knowledge of the demand curve is probably enjoyed by no firm that can influence market price. (Excellent general discussions of the lack-of-information problem are provided by Richardson [102], Clark [20], Andrews [62] and Shackle [103].)

One simple way round the problem is to assume that firms make estimates of the future trends of important variables and perhaps use a range of estimates ('best', 'worst' and 'most likely'), looking at the profits which would result from each possible outcome. Better still, we can assume they attach probabilities to these outcomes. They could then use expected values in maximisation calculations. It is known that some larger firms operate in this way, but most know little of probability theory and less about techniques for maximising profit. None the less, Machlup ([104, [105]) has argued that businessmen can achieve by intuition what economists get by analysis. But he does concede that they could operate only on the basis of their own *subjective* guesses about demand and costs. There is therefore no reason to believe they get the same results as traditional theory which uses correct *objective* data.

Unfortunately, once we introduce risk and uncertainty there is no longer a unique correct decision. A project may have a positive *expected value* but there may be some chance of making a loss. The firm may reject the project because it does not want to risk the loss. And if it dislikes gambles involving losses, rejection may be rational. Yet another firm which likes a gamble might accept under the same conditions. Much depends on the firm's attitude towards risk. For an introduction to the formal analysis of decision-making under risk and uncertainty, see [106] or [107].

Once uncertainty is admitted, stockholding becomes especially important. It will pay the firm to hold stocks so that in periods of unexpected excess demand it will not have to turn away profitable sales. It may also pay it not to cut production in periods of temporary set-backs in demand but instead to produce for stock. The effect of incorporating uncertainty and stockholding into price/output models has not, so far, been very extensively explored. But for a major attempt at the problem and a good bibliography of 'inventory' models see Mills [108], and for a critique see Steuer and Budd [109].

GAME THEORY

A powerful new method of analysing the wide range of possible outcomes under oligopoly was developed by von Neumann and Morgenstern [110]. In the first flush of early optimism many economists believed 'game theory' would provide general determinate solutions to the oligopoly problem. Although this optimism has not been justified by later developments, game theory has taught us to understand the problem better.

The basic approach in game theory is to construct a payoff matrix showing how firms A and B fare under various strategies. In the simplest model, whatever A gains, B loses, and this is termed a 'zero-sum game'. The payoff matrix (Table 1)

Table 1

PAYOFF MATRIX

		B's strategies		
		X	Y	Z
A's strategies	X	+100	0	−100
	Y	+200	−50	−200
	Z	+300	+50	+ 20

shows the gains or losses for A of various strategies. The effect on B is easily deduced, since whatever A gains, B loses. For example, assume three new advertising media can be used: X, Y or Z. If A uses X, and B does as well, A gains 100 so

56

B loses 100. But if B uses Y when A uses X, both firms gain nothing.

If firm A is cautious, it may look at the worst that could happen to it with each of its three possible strategies. If it adopts X it could lose £100 (if B chooses strategy Z); if it adopts Y it could lose £200; and if it adopts Z the worst that could happen is that it makes an extra £20. The best of the worst outcomes from A's point of view (the maximum minimorum or maximin) is therefore +20, so it adopts strategy Z. On the other hand, if firm B is cautious it will look for the worst of the best outcomes for A (the minimum maximorum or minimax), since A's gain is B's loss. If B chooses strategy X he could lose £300 to A; if he chooses Y he could lose £50 and if Z he loses £20 to A. So B chooses Z as his minimax strategy. In this example both firms do what the other firm expected and there is a stable solution (strategy Z for both firms) which is called a 'saddle-point'.

But not all games have so simple a solution. And in particular, most industrial problems are not of the zero-sum type. Zero-sum implies that all policies being considered gain for A exactly what B loses. But often different policies have different effects. For example, if both firms put up price they may *both* be better off. And we are now in the complex area of 'non-constant-sum' games.

If we introduce more firms the problem becomes more complex still, and we need 'n-person non-constant-sum' games which can become technically difficult enough to suggest that few firms in practice are behaving in such a sophisticated and complex way. It is enough to say that minimax may no longer be the most profitable strategy. It may involve lower profits than Cournot-type behaviour and far lower profits than joint profit maximisation.

None the less, if we take a simplified example with two firms who are considering only two possible prices, the oligopoly problem is brought sharply into focus. Consider Table 2. If firm A charges £2 the worst that could happen is that it will make only £75 profit (if B chooses a price of £1). But if A chooses £1 the worst that can happen is profits of £100. So

Table 2

PRICE STRATEGIES

		B's price			
		£1		£2	
		A's profit	B's profit	A's profit	B's profit
A's price	£1	100	100	250	75
	£2	75	250	200	200

the £1 price is preferred as a maximin strategy. Exactly the same reasoning would lead B to a price of £1. Even if we forget maximin, whatever price A chooses it always pays B to cut its price to £1; similarly, whatever price B chooses it pays A to cut its price to £1. Yet paradoxically both would make more profit if they both charged £2 (profits of £200 each). This game is of the classic prisoners' dilemma type (see Luce and Raiffa [111]).

But the problem here is partly due to the single-move nature of the game. The problem is akin to tendering for a contract. You can offer one price only and do not know your competitors' quotes. But most pricing problems are not like this. Having made one move and received a response, you can change your price. If sequences of moves are allowed, the firms in Table 2 may well both adopt the joint profit-maximising price of £2. If A sets £2 to begin with, B can reason that it pays him to cut his price to £1 *only if A will keep his price of £2*. But A will not. Once B charges £1 it pays A to do so as well. So B may decide not to charge £1 but to charge £2 as A has done. It pays them both. And if A reasons that B will reason like this, it pays A to charge £2 and not the maximin price of £1. But the problem is there. A can work out his best move only by guessing what B will do. And he can guess what B will do only if he knows what B guesses A will do in response. It is the tedious problem of 'I know that he knows that I know that he knows . . .'.

In practice, the guessing problem can be simplified by industrial spying, or by collusion, or by learning from experience that life is more comfortable if all move prices together, perhaps by accepting a price leader. Alternatively, firms which step out of line may face ferocious competition to discourage them from doing it in future. In a dynamic situation there are many ways to learn over time an acceptable way of living with a complicated problem. And many industries have emerged from initial bouts of cut-throat competition into a more mature stage of relative stability of prices.

Game theory has not yet come up with general solutions to the oligopoly problem. But it has highlighted what the problem is and has shown some of the avenues open to firms to make the problem less daunting than it at first appears. It has also provided a useful guide to government policy in some spheres. For example, it highlights the importance of having monopoly legislation to restrict collusion via cartels, information agreements and the like. The less the collusion the greater the likelihood that the low minimax price will prevail and the smaller the chance of the joint profit-maximisation position being reached. The importance of controlling concentration is also shown. The more firms there are the harder it is to guess what everyone else will do, and again minimax prices are made more likely.

A certain amount of experimenting has been done by facing subjects with game-theory payoff matrices based on oligopoly pricing problems. These suggest a tendency to learn from experience to pick the joint profit-maximising price, though the tendency is weaker the more firms there are and the more unequal are different firms' costs and demand conditions. Joint maximisation is also made less likely by reducing the amount of information the participants have about each other's price/output decisions and profits (see Fouraker and Siegel [112] and Friedman [113]).

Von Neumann and Morgenstern incorporated into game theory the benefits, under certain conditions, of leaving the choice of decision purely to chance, e.g. by tossing a coin. For a clear introduction to this and other aspects of game theory, see Baumol [114] and [39] and Shubik [115].

5 Alternative Models to Profit Maximisation

Aside from doubts about whether firms have the information to maximise profits, there has been widespread uncertainty as to whether they would want to maximise profits even if they could.

To argue that all firms aim to do nothing else but maximise profits has no better basis in logic or intuition than to argue that all students aim only to maximise examination marks. The utility of beer, sport, politics, music and the like would be ignored, as would the fact that time spent on pleasures must be traded for time in the lecture-room and library. So too in industry. The utility of profits must be traded – where it conflicts – with prestige buildings, donations to charity, empire-building, big company cars, attractive but dim-witted secretaries, long expensive lunches and the host of other features of industrial life which may be enjoyable but which do not always increase profits in the way that theory demands.

To say that a man maximises profits means in practical terms that nothing – absolutely nothing – which conflicts with profit yields him any utility at all. He would sack 10,000 men and all his relatives and friends if it would make him a farthing of extra profit, even if he was already making £100 million worth a year. He would work in a damp, dingy office and drive round in a second-hand rubbish truck – if it helped profit by however little. He would cheat, lie and risk the lives of millions of people if only it would make his firm a few extra pennies. He would break every moral he had, however strong his belief. He would make Al Capone seem like a benevolent uncle.

As for size, if there were no difference in profits, he would as soon have the firm of which he was chairman be so small that none of us had ever heard of it as have it be the largest firm the world had ever known. The entrepreneur in traditional economics is, in short, a quite extraordinary man.

In fairness to profit-maximising models, it should be borne in mind that they were originally designed for the age of the entrepreneur who owned and managed the business, who took all the decisions and took for himself all the profits that resulted from them. While no one believed that profit was his sole motivation, many did feel it was a sufficiently dominant motive to give us a worthwhile *approximation* of his behaviour.

A further argument was that even if firms did not *aim* to maximise profits, they would none the less be *forced* to do so in the long run by pressure of market forces. And given the assumption of free entry, this was a tenable argument. New entrants would eventually force firms to maximise profits or go bankrupt, since in equilibrium normal profits are possible only at the maximum profits position. In the long run it is a case of 'survival of the fittest' (see Alchian [116] and Winter [117]). But the dramatically increased levels of concentration over the last century (see Utton [90]) and the evidence on barriers to free entry (see Chapter 4) make this market forces argument seem rather old-fashioned.

As for the dependence of theory on the entrepreneur, the arrival of joint-stock companies and the near-total division of ownership and control between shareholders and managers has produced an obvious need to rethink the motivation of today's decision-makers ([119]–[123]). In the U.S.A., for example, ownership groups now have a majority holding of shares in only five of the top 200 companies (Larner [121]). Today's decision-makers do not get the profits: they get a salary and other forms of job satisfaction. And like humans in all other areas of economics they probably try to maximise their own welfare, which is no longer necessarily synonymous with that of the firm. If it were not so, no employee would steal, or shirk, or make private telephone calls in the firm's time at the firm's expense. For a development of the shirking and pilfering problems and the attendant costs of detection and measurement, see Alchian and Demsetz [118].

Disillusionment with profit maximisation has led to new models of firms being developed which concentrate on other aspects from which utility may be derived (e.g. output, sales revenue and staff). These are the first exploratory steps towards utility maximisation. So far it must be admitted that they are only tentative, held back by an awareness that a full-blown utility model can produce any answer we want depending on the relative weighting of the variables we care to include. So the new theories have tried to widen the neo-classical profit motive to make it complex enough to be fairly realistic yet simple enough to provide definite results. The search is for a simplified general approximation of firms' behaviour and not for a precise mirror-image of any particular firm.

The major alternative approaches to profit maximisation are outlined below to give some idea of the range of types of model in use in economics today.

UTILITY MAXIMISATION

In one of the earliest attempts to push the theory of the firm towards utility maximisation, Papandreou [124] criticised the emphasis in economics on firms as entrepreneurs rather than as organisations. The objective of an organisation would come about as a result of internal and external pressures and would be some kind of amalgam of the preferences of the various sections of the organisation. There would be a 'general preference function'. Papandreou did not develop a model, but pointed out the problem of getting definite results from general preference functions unless we could specify their form and measure them.

Scitovsky, too [125], helped the move away from profits as a firm's sole motive. In particular, he was worried about the trade-off between entrepreneurial effort and profit and showed that entrepreneurs would maximise profit only if their choice between more income and more leisure was independent of their income, i.e. the supply of entrepreneurship must have zero income elasticity.

Perhaps one of the best examples of a formal utility-maximising model has been provided by Williamson [126]–[129]. Management, he believes, will be interested not only in profit but also in the number of staff under their control. The empire-building motive is catered for by including expenditure on staff (S) in the utility function. More staff are valued because they lead to the manager getting more salary, more prestige and more security. In addition, management are interested in 'managerial slack' (M), e.g. 'perks' such as a plush office, a big expense account, company cars and on-the-job leisure. Finally, they like to have funds available to them for discretionary investment (ID) which is not economically strictly essential.

Armed with these beliefs, Williamson sets up various models in which managers maximise utility functions such as:

$$U = U\ (S,M,ID)$$

subject to the constraint that after-tax profits are big enough to pay satisfactory dividends and pay for economically necessary (as opposed to discretionary) investments.

An interesting feature of the equilibrium conditions for the model is that for its chosen optimum staff level the firm will equate marginal cost and marginal revenue with respect to a change in output, i.e. in equilibrium

$$\frac{\partial R}{\partial X} = \frac{\partial C}{\partial X}$$

where R = total revenue, C = total cost and X = output.

But this is not the same as profit maximisation, in that the level of staff at which the marginal cost and revenue of output are equated is non-optimal from the profit point of view so that output levels may differ. The utility-maximising firm spends more on staff than is justified by profits so that

63

$\partial R / \partial S < 1$, whereas a profit-maximiser would stop where $\partial R / \partial S = 1$.

Exploring the implications of the model, Williamson finds that firms who maximise his concept of utility will (*a*) increase output and staff expenditure if the profit-tax rate increases (the utility of profits is reduced by the higher tax rate, so managers seek utility elsewhere by buying extra staff and output), and (*b*) reduce output and staff expenditure if a lump-sum tax is imposed (they must go back towards the profit-maximising level since the lump-sum tax makes it harder to meet the profit constraint).

By contrast, lump-sum taxes and changes in profits tax have no effect on profit-maximisers. However, increased demand causes both firms to raise output and spend more on staff, though Williamson's firm will increase managerial slack the easier it is to make profits. This last conclusion is important and backed by empirical evidence. It is a fairly typical response of firms in tough times, that they go on a diet in terms of managerial slack.

There are many parallels between some of Williamson's arguments and Leibenstein's arguments for X-inefficiency. Since Leibenstein argues that employees maximise their own utility, not the firm's profits, and yield inefficiencies as a result, one could argue that his is at least in part a utility-maximising theory. X-inefficiency can, of course, be incorporated in all models, not just in profit-maximisation.

Without much ingenuity one could put most theories into a utility format, e.g. we could argue that for revenue-maximisers utility is a function of sales revenue.

SALES REVENUE MAXIMISATION

The separation of ownership from control and the link between salaries and sales (see Roberts [130] and McGuire *et al.* [131]) were among many factors which led Baumol ([39], [132], [133]) to believe that managers were more likely to be interested in maximising sales than profits. In particular, he thought their interest would centre on sales value rather than volume (if only because maximum volume involves a zero price – giving the product away free). Maximising sales revenue involves choosing the price/output level where marginal revenue is zero (i.e. no price cut would increase sales value so that the firm is at the peak of its total revenue (sales value) curve).

So simple a motivation is not, however, adequate. At the level of output where revenue was maximised, costs might exceed revenue and the company would make a loss. Baumol accepted that some profits were necessary for survival: managers, he thought, would have in mind a constraint level of profit which would be just enough to keep shareholders happy and make it possible to borrow funds to finance future growth. The company's motivation was therefore to maximise sales revenue subject to profits being at least equal to the constraint level. Diagrammatically this is shown in Fig. 9.

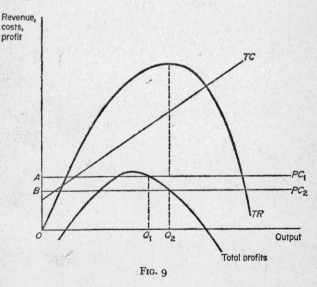

FIG. 9

Sales revenue is maximised (TR is at a peak) at output Q_2 and, if it can, the company will choose this output level. Its profits would be OB. Whether or not it can choose this output level depends on the size of the profit constraint. If the constraint is OB, then output Q_2 can be chosen where revenue is maximised. It will just be possible to earn the constraint level of profits.

If, however, the constraint is higher than OB, then the firm will have to reduce output to make adequate profits, e.g. if the profit constraint is PC_1 the company will have to reduce output to Q_1 in order to meet the constraint. It will not be able to maximise revenue, but this is the best it can do since no lower output yields as much revenue as output Q_1; and no higher output yields enough profits to meet the constraint. But what happens if the constraint is less than OB, i.e. below the level of PC_2? It would then be possible to produce beyond Q_2, but the firm would not do so as this is the revenue-maximising output. Constraints below PC_2 are therefore ineffective; the company can maximise revenue while earning profits above the minimum level required.

Baumol, however, has argued that the constraint will always be effective because the company can always use any surplus profits to advertise and increase its revenue. In Fig. 10, for example, the profit-maximiser will spend OA on advertising

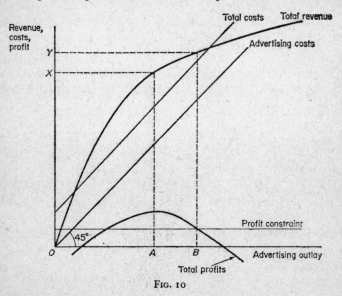

FIG. 10

and have OX of total revenue, while a revenue-maximiser with the profit constraint shown would spend OB on advertising and have OY of revenue.

Baumol has drawn some interesting conclusions from his model. He has shown that if fixed costs (overheads, etc.) increase in the short run, then revenue-maximisers will increase price and reduce output (the higher costs prevent their making the constraint level of profits unless they move back nearer to the maximum profits position), whereas, as is well known, the profit-maximiser's price/output levels remain unchanged. *MC = MR* He also concludes that revenue-maximisers will in general produce and advertise more than profit-maximisers.

The revenue-maximisation model has led to much interest and much dispute. Shepherd [134] claimed that in oligopoly the firm would be faced by kinked demand curves and that if the kink was severe enough revenue and profits could be maximised at the same output level. But Shepherd's conclusions have been shown by Hawkins [135] not to hold if advertising or any other form of non-price competition (packaging, give-aways, service, etc.) is possible – which it normally is.

It has also been shown (Hawkins [136]) that the conclusion that a revenue-maximiser will in general produce and advertise more than a profit-maximiser is invalid. He may choose a higher, lower or identical output – and a higher, lower or identical advertising budget. It depends on the responsiveness of demand to advertising rather than price cuts. This conclusion holds for firms producing only one product, or one group of products.

Where firms produce many products, as is fairly typical nowadays, then in the static model revenue and profit maximisation yield the same results [135]. Baumol, however, has developed a growth model of sales revenue maximisation which Williamson has shown to yield different results from profit maximisation.

On the motivation of revenue-maximisers, Rosenberg [137] has questioned its plausibility and Peston [138] has looked at some of the implications of a more general approach where revenue and profit both form part of the firm's utility function.

67

As for empirical testing of Baumol's model, nothing very conclusive has yet emerged (see Hall [139], Waverman [140], and Mabry and Siders [141]).

Revenue maximisation is certainly one of the most important – some would argue *the* most important – of the alternatives to profit maximisation. The interest it has attracted is no doubt partly due to its being presented very much in the mould of the traditional models, and to its explicit incorporation of advertising (surely important in any modern theory aiming at practical relevance). But it is also attractive as a model because it has been fruitful of interesting results and has *prima facie* plausibility in this age of manager-dominated, advertising-conscious giant corporations.

Even if, under certain circumstances, revenue and profit maximisation lead to essentially similar results, the model may still have provided an interesting insight into managerial motivation.

OUTPUT MAXIMISATION

A fairly obvious alternative to maximising the *value* of sales is instead to maximise their *volume*, i.e. to maximise output. Ames [142] has argued that output maximisation is an acceptable simplification of the motive of most Soviet enterprises, since 'Soviet enterprises and the Soviet press say that enterprises exist in order to produce at least as much (and if possible more) than state plans call for'. He admits the theory is a simple one, but argues that 'until a simple theory clearly breaks down, it is preferable to a complicated one'. Kafoglis [143] suggests that output maximisation with a profit constraint may fit the motives of some private firms and also of public services who may be judged by output but told to 'break even'.

It is difficult to get much of interest out of output maximisation since it merely implies that firms choose that level of output where the demand and cost curves cross, i.e. where $AC = AR$. Obviously, where $MC > AC$ (decreasing returns to scale) this implies output beyond the Pareto-optimal position (where $MC=AR$) and, equally obviously, labour will be employed (as will other factors) up to the point where their price equals their average product. Pareto-optimal output can, however, result if firms operate on the base of a flat L-shaped cost curve, i.e. where $AC=MC$. This follows because at maximum output, subject to breaking even, $AC=AR$; and since $AC=MC$ it follows that $MC=AR$ as in perfect competition.

Kafoglis explores the effects of the firm being able to charge different prices in different markets, and Ames looks at the effect of the firm having a utility function which contains output and profits (the result is that price and output are between the profit-maximising and break-even levels; exactly where between the two levels depends on the relative preference for profits rather than output).

Just how far output maximisation can be developed is not yet known. But a major problem arises if the firm is multi-product. It is interesting to ponder how we can add up a firm's output of refrigerators, biscuits and cars. Certainly, we could add up the *value* of the sales of each product, but the model would then merge indissolubly into a model of sales revenue maximisation.

CONSTRAINED OUTPUT AND PROFIT MAXIMISATION

One model which has been shown to yield interesting results and which has links with output maximisation is that of Averch and Johnson [144]. They examined the implications of firms (such as public utilities) being constrained to make no more than a specified rate of return on capital. Although scarcely an alternative theory of the firm – perhaps more a special case of other theories – the model is included here partly because of its links with output maximisation and partly because it has important implications – especially in public-sector economics.

In one of its extreme forms the model yields the same

results as output maximisation, i.e. if the constraint rate of profit is set to equal normal profits, then the firm maximises output and breaks even (see Kafoglis [143]). At the other extreme (when the constraint rate of return is so high that it cannot be achieved at any price/output level), the firm may maximise profits in the conventional way or pursue any other motive it may care to select. Between these two extremes, constrained profit-maximisers will

(a) increase their capital stock the more the maximum allowable rate of return is reduced towards the market rate of interest;

(b) produce more output than unregulated firms; and

(c) will not minimise cost at their chosen output level.

Essentially what happens is that, since the firm is constrained as to the rate of return it can make on capital invested, it will invest more capital than unregulated firms so as to increase *absolute* profits while abiding by the rule about *rates* of profit. It will therefore use more capital and less labour than is consistent with minimising costs at ruling market prices. These conclusions have been most simply derived by Stein and Borts [145], who also list some useful further reading.

BEHAVIOURAL THEORIES

Few would doubt that behavioural theories are among the most dramatic of the new approaches to the theory of the firm. What is dramatic is that they dispense with the assumption that firms aim to maximise anything – even utility.

The basis of the behaviourist approach is that instead of hypothesising about how rational men respond to various situations or saying how they should respond, we should instead study how firms really do take decisions in practice. From this evidence it is hoped we can use logical argument to develop theories of behaviour relevant to a wide range of firms other than just the initial ones we have studied.

As an example of the approach, Simon ([146]–[149]) has

argued that most psychological theories assume that instead of maximising, people normally *satisfice*. And there is evidence to support this view. Instead of aiming at maximum profits, he argues, we should assume firms aspire to a satisfactory level or rate of profit. Research has shown (for references, see Simon [146]) that if performance falls short of the aspiration level, a search begins for alternative ways of achieving it. And at the same time, the aspiration level is adjusted down to levels more likely to be achieved. Simon quotes cost-plus pricing as a form of satisficing which has empirical backing.

The second major basis of full-scale behavioural theories (almost all theories have *some* behavioural content) is the belief that we can no longer look at firms as having one major decision-maker (e.g. the entrepreneur), but instead we must look at them as complex organisations. The problem then is that organisational theories do not accept one goal as being relevant. More typically they expect different parts of the organisation to have different goals (e.g. production, inventory, sales, market-share and profit goals). There may be conflict between these goals which needs resolving within the firm, which is seen therefore as a coalition of conflicting interests. The organisation searches for information (which is costly) on how well it is meeting its various goals and responds to the information it gets. Having specified the nature of the search activity, the responses, the information, the goals and so on, a computer program can be set up to simulate how the firm behaves through time in response to varying conditions.

Cyert and March [150] have devised a behavioural model of duopoly. Each firm estimates demand and production costs and chooses its output level. If this output level will not yield the aspired level of profit, it searches for ways to reduce costs, re-estimates demand and, if need be, lowers its profit target. The other firm behaves in a similar way. By feeding in data on demand, costs, market share and the like, and by using computer simulation, it was possible to compare the model's predictions with the behaviour of the duopoly market shared by the American Can Company and the Continental Can

71

Company. Most of the important moves by the two companies were predicted remarkably well by the model. Baumol and Stewart [151] have achieved similarly satisfactory results using this behavioural model.

A detailed outline of behavioural theory and the empirical evidence on which it is based is given in Cyert and March [150], and is summarised by Cohen and Cyert [152].

For another example of the behavioural approach see Cyert and Kamien [153], and for an interesting model based on the problems of passing information through a large bureaucracy, see Monsen and Downs [154]; the latter, though not a behavioural model, is an example of the sort of problem we might ultimately want to incorporate into any behavioural approach. Assessments of behavioural versus other approaches to the theory of the firm are provided by Machlup [105], Margolis [155] and briefly by Archibald [156]. For an interesting and very persuasively argued viewpoint on the influence that the behavioural approach could have on the theory of the firm, see Clarkson [157].

Criticism of the behavioural approach is along the lines that it uses a sledgehammer to crack a walnut. Do we really need to construct mirror-images of companies, virtually assembling the decision-making process brick by brick, in order to predict their behaviour? Would not simpler models suffice for the limited purposes we have in mind? The staunchest defender of profit maximisation along these lines has been Machlup ([104], [105]) and there is much worth reading in his argument. One of his major points is that

Even if formal accuracy demanded that we accept the maximisation of the decision-maker's total utility as the basic assumption, simplicity and fruitfulness speak for sticking with the postulate of maximisation of money profits for situations in which competition is effective. The question is not whether the firms of the real world will *really* maximise profits, or whether they even *strive* to maximise their money profits, but rather whether the *assumption* that this is the objective of the theoretical firms in the artificial world of our construction will lead to conclusions very different from those derived from admittedly more realistic assumptions.

He goes on to argue that 'some of the "realistic assumptions" proposed for inclusion in the theory can affect (by an unknown amount) the magnitude but not the direction of any change that is likely to result from a specified change in conditions'. None the less, he does concede that in welfare economics at least we are interested in predicting more than just the direction of change. We need precise relationships such as '$MC = AR$ for all firms' or 'Labour is paid its marginal physical product'. These relationships cannot be derived *correctly* except by having completely realistic theories of firms' behaviour. And in markets where competition is not completely effective (e.g. in oligopoly), as Machlup himself concedes, managerial discretion may alter not just the extent of change but also its direction, as the Williamson model has clearly demonstrated.

There is therefore a case for behavioural theories – for building models of firms brick by brick. And eventually we may be able to simplify them radically without contradicting their predictions. Or such is the hope.

COST-PLUS PRICING

So far, the most empirically supported theory of pricing is the 'cost-plus' theory. There are in fact, many cost-plus theories but they have a common basis: firms set price by estimating production costs and adding on a 'mark-up' for profit. Some firms add the mark-up to variable costs, others to fixed costs, others to full (or total) costs. And some add it to various accountancy definitions of cost which do not convert directly to an economist's treatment of the subject. But the methods are essentially similar: though the cost base may vary, if the cost element is small the mark-up is big and vice versa. There are almost as many names for cost-plus pricing as there are methods of carrying it out: the main alternatives used are 'full-cost', 'mark-up', 'administered' or 'target' pricing.

The first article on the subject was published in 1939 by

Hall and Hitch [56]. It gave evidence for kinked demand curves as well as for believing that firms set price on a mark-up basis. Since then a mass of supporting evidence has been accumulated. For an excellent survey article see Heflebower [158], and for other evidence see Andrews [62], Wiles [81], Clark [20], Kaplan et al. [43], Markham [159], Fog [160], Lanzillotti [161], Haynes [162], Pearce [163] and the N.B.E.R. studies ([85] and [86]).

One problem for cost-plus pricing is that production costs may vary with output. It is then necessary to forecast output in order to derive the cost base. In practice, firms often use output in the previous period or a 'standard' output (e.g. x per cent of current capacity) and then add on a mark-up to yield them their desired return on capital. This sort of system is commonplace, not just in Britain but also on a worldwide basis. And its use has been verified in every size of company from the smallest right up to General Motors (see the Senate Report on Automobiles [164]).

But why is cost-plus pricing used? It is after all not enough just to say that in practice it is used, since no motivation is implied. And until the motivation is known there is no way of predicting firms' responses to varying conditions or of knowing why they choose any particular size of mark-up.

Two main arguments have been put forward as the reasons for the widespread use of cost-plus pricing. One is that firms are 'satisficers', not 'maximisers', i.e. they aim to make a reasonable level of profit, not the maximum possible level. Associated with this argument is the belief that some firms want only a 'fair' or 'just' rate of profit. Too much is immoral. No doubt there are some people, perhaps many, who have moral feelings about the level of profit they should earn and like to offer good value for money. But the bulk of the evidence suggests that the size of the 'plus' margin varies: it grows in boom times and it varies with elasticity of demand and barriers to entry. See, as examples, Hall and Hitch [56], Fog [160] and Kaplan et al. [43]. It seems strange that people's concept of a 'fair' profit should generally vary so systematically with the ease of making profits.

74

None the less, varying the profit margin is consistent with 'satisficing' behaviour where once a level of profit has been achieved people may raise the level which they expect to make. And if it cannot be achieved they may lower their aspiration level, as Simon has suggested [146].

Even though firms who cost-plus may respond to changes in demand, they do not seem to do so in a short-run profit-maximising way. Jaguar Cars, for example, when they announced their XJ12 model, were faced with considerable excess demand and long order-books. Not only did they not raise price to equate supply and demand and boost short-run profits, but they also announced they were trying to stop speculators buying the car and selling it at a profit in the second-hand market. Second-hand prices were at times reported as being £1,500 higher than the new price. Similar policies were pursued by car manufacturers during the shortage after the Second World War.

But care must be taken in assessing motives for behaviour of this type. Some would argue that increasing the price would discourage long-run demand, reduce customer goodwill and would look like exploitation. The excess demand may be only temporary and price might need to be lowered again in the near future.

And this is the second major reason given for cost-plus pricing. It is argued that in an uncertain world where perfect information is lacking, demand cannot be accurately forecast for this month or this year, let alone for a few years hence. And today's price policy may affect demand far into the future. Nor can firms, in practice, estimate all the permutations of all the variables that should be looked at to derive the optimum price. The number of permutations may run into billions even on a simple problem (see Baumol [114] and Clarkson [157]), so that no computer could readily digest them, let alone a manager during a two-hour meeting at which a dozen other decisions must be taken as well. As an example, to calculate the optimum price for all the thousands of items sold by a typical department store would be a *costly* process (even if adequate information could be obtained). Bearing these costs in mind, it may well be better to apply a standard mark-up, to all items, which is known from experience to work reasonably well. This suffices as a first approximation (see Cyert and March [150] pp. 146–7, for an example). The company can then aim to supply all that is demanded at this cost-plus price. It can use stocks to cushion the effects of unexpected short-run fluctuations in demand. And over a period of time it may decide to vary the mark-up in response to changing conditions (booms, slumps, strength of competition and so on), to experiment and learn from experience. Firms may therefore see cost-plus as the best they can do, in the long run, in a complex uncertain world where conditions are continually changing. Whether or not long-run profits are ever achieved at anything like the potential maximum depends, of course, on the skill of the practitioners in responding to continuously changing circumstances.

Two other features of cost-plus pricing are worth noting. One is the strong link with entry-forestalling behaviour already noted (see Chapter 4). The second is the way that cost-plus pricing can ameliorate the problem of competitors' reactions in oligopoly. It can effectively lead to tacit collusion. Once all the firms have got used to the size of mark-up which is being generally applied in their industry, they can predict each other's price changes in response to changing conditions such as cost increases. Long after governments have broken up a price ring, the fact that the firms are used to a conventional mark-up may lead to their prices staying closely in line without any formal collusion. Firms may, in fact, adopt cost-plus pricing partly for the very reason that they recognise the oligopoly problem, dislike the prospect of price wars and accept the need for a 'community of outlook' (Cyert and March [150]).

There is little dispute that empirical evidence strongly supports the view that cost-plus is the most common method used for setting prices in practice. There is, however, much dispute about the usefulness of this information until we have much more evidence on the motivation of the firms who use the method. After all, there is no reason why short-run profit-maximisers, long-run profit-maximisers and revenue-maximisers should not all use cost-plus as a *means* of setting price. They could all, however, choose different mark-ups in order to meet their objectives.

And to some extent this is reflected in the names of the various cost-plus theories. 'Full-cost pricing' is applied to firms who want to cover costs including only a normal rate of return on capital, while 'target pricing' is usually applied to firms who aim to make a chosen return on capital which exceeds the 'normal' rate of return as defined by economic theory. For discussion of the different approaches, see Clark [20].

Since the size of the mark-up depends on the firm's objectives, evidence on motivation is clearly crucial. But finding out what really does motivate managers is unfortunately an extremely difficult task which is currently far from complete. Interviews are not beyond suspicion since what people say they are doing may not be what they are doing. And it is possible that none of us can correctly assess our own motivations. As an example of the difficulties, Lanzillotti [161], after interviewing many large American companies, concluded that profit was not their dominant motive. Yet a majority of these same companies, when asked about pricing, said that they did not think that changing price would increase their long-run profits.

GROWTH MODELS

A number of models have been developed which suggest that management derives utility from growth. Marris [165], for example, has suggested that growth will be a major objective of management. Increasing the growth rate is argued to be costly in terms of profits so that more and more growth may depress the stock-market value of the company below the level that could potentially be gained. Fear of being taken over, if stock-market value is too far depressed, might prevent a total commitment to growth, as might concern over shareholders' welfare. So a link between growth rates and share prices was needed, and Marris develops this (most simply in

77

[166]) by using a 'steady-state' growth model. It is assumed that once the growth rate is established (which stays constant through time), all the main variables (sales, profits, assets, etc.) grow at the given rate. But the firm can choose between many different growth rates. Higher growth rates will involve more time and effort (and therefore expense) in searching for profitable ventures, may involve more advertising to increase demand and more research and development. So the higher the growth rate the higher the proportion of current profits which will have to be retained to finance these growth-promoting activities, and to finance the investment needed for extra capacity.

Retaining more profits to finance faster growth necessarily reduces the current dividend, which harms the share price. But the higher growth rate achieved implies that dividends also grow at this higher rate. This should boost the share price. To summarise: increasing the growth rate has two effects with opposite results on the share price – the lower current dividend decreases the value of the shares, while the higher growth rate increases it. These two effects need not exactly balance. Marris shows that eventually higher growth rates will have a net depressing effect on share prices,[1] and as a result when firms select a growth rate they are also selecting a market valuation. Owing to the separation of ownership from control, there is no reason why managers should pick the best market value from the shareholder's point of view. They may instead pick the best growth rate from their own point of view: they may, for example, pick the highest growth rate which does not depress the market value below the level at which the company would be taken over. For to be taken over might involve many managers losing their jobs. Or, if their utility depends on the company's market value and on the growth rate, then (depending on the shape of their indifference curves) management may choose a growth rate somewhere between the rate that maximises market value and the rate at which takeover would take place.

[1] At high enough growth rates all profits will have to be retained; there will be no dividend ever, and share prices will fall to zero.

An alternative growth model has been developed by Baumol [167] in which he explores the implications of firms wanting to maximise the growth rate of sales revenue. This model has been extended by J. H. Williamson [168] to compare the results of maximising profits, growth and sales. Among the more interesting results that Williamson derives are that:

(a) Growth will be limited by the fear of takeover as Marris has claimed and not by lack of funds as Baumol claimed.

(b) The static sales-maximisation model cannot be derived from growth maximisation but it can be derived from long-run sales maximisation.

(c) Profit- and growth-maximisers choose the same output levels but a sales-maximiser will produce more.

All the growth models of firms assume that expansion costs money and that the faster the growth rate the more expansion will cost. This is necessary to stop firms doing everything that is profitable at once. The case for this assumption was originally made by Penrose [100] and has been discussed at length by Marris [165].

The problem with growth models of firms at their present stage is that they massively simplify the problem in order to make it manageable. Cost and revenue schedules are assumed not to shift through time, factor prices and the rate of interest are held constant, firms are assumed to have unlimited scope to sell extra output without cutting prices (e.g. by diversifying) and it is assumed that all major variables such as profits, sales and costs will increase at the same rate. It is also assumed that firms can take decisions (e.g. about prices) independently and ignore the problem of oligopolistic interdependence.

As for the motivation aspect, one might question why firms would want the growth rate to be constant (they might prefer to grow faster now and less fast later). And we might also question whether, in a world where even the simple techniques of maximising profits are argued to be largely unknown, firms are likely to be using the level of technique needed to solve a steady-state growth model. There is also grave doubt as to whether they would have now – or ever – the data necessary for the task.

But we have so far seen only the opening moves in this new approach to the theory of the firm. And the models are bound to be over-simplified at this stage.

One last point – which is not a criticism of growth models but a condition for their existence – is that the basic assumption behind all these models is the imperfect operation of the capital market. In a 'perfect' market any firm which pursued growth in a way that depressed its market value below the level that could be achieved would be taken over. The growth rate at which takeover would take place would be any rate different from that which maximised profits, and no other motivation could be pursued. The fundamental problem, of course, is that neither shareholders, brokers nor those who might take the firm over have perfect knowledge of just how high profits could potentially be. For a wide-ranging discussion of the factors behind the market imperfections, see Marris ([165] and [166]), and for some empirical tests which suggest that there is a greater likelihood of takeover when share prices are depressed relative to book value, see Kuehn [169] and Singh and Whittington [170].

6 Conclusion

Profit maximisation, the economist's suit for all occasions, has now begun to be replaced by a wardrobe of theories. That they seem all to be based on different motivations and different methods of operation within firms – and to yield different results – may well be confusing. But to regret the proliferation of theories of the firm is clearly futile. It was a necessary price to pay for added realism. But now that new knowledge of the complexity of the behaviour of firms has made us less able to provide the simple universal relationships (like marginal cost equals price) which are needed for welfare theory and the other branches of economics, has the need to formulate coherent theories of the firm been correspondingly devalued? After all, one of the main reasons for studying firms was to find such relationships, between cost and price, between the output of labour and its wage, and so on – relationships which were assumed to hold universally and which could therefore be held to apply throughout economic theory. If the credibility of such universal relationships is now severely strained, has the study of firms any real point?

It must be stressed, first, that this inability to find valid universal relationships is not a failure of theory, of technique, understanding or effort: it is just that the problem has turned out to be vastly more complex than was at first imagined. Recognising the wide range of types of firm now in existence, allowing for the enormous size range that our concept of a firm must now cover, from the local newsagent right up to multinational, multi-product giants like I.C.I. and Unilever, and considering the whole gamut of motivations which can be

81

and are being followed by the several hundred thousand owners, directors, managers and workers all involved in one large bureaucratic organisation, it would be surprising – not to say miraculous – if any simple formula existed, even for one firm, which remained invariant over time. And even if it did, it is surely almost beyond belief that such a formula could also hold without modification for every other firm in the economy as well.

But this does not mean that the study of firms is no longer of use. Aside from the hope that some vestigial truth of the universal kind we once sought may yet be found – a hope which some still retain in the face of every discouragement – aside from this lingering hope there are a number of reasons, less spectacular admittedly but requiring no apology, for pursuing the study of firms. Micro-economics does not just consist of discussions about social welfare and of saying what should happen. It also has an important role to play in addressing the general arguments derived from theory to a vast range of problems – from simple ones such as the price a parent company should charge subsidiaries for its products, if it wants to maximise profits, right through to complex issues like optimal investment strategy under conditions of uncertainty and capital rationing. Economic theory of this kind is of value in business and managerial economics, in commerce and accountancy, and many other fields. One could say that here the role of the theory of the firm has the same relationship to the management of firms as does much of macro-economics to governments in their running of the economy as a whole.

The link with macro-economics is of course much stronger than merely one of analogy. There is no doubt that the micro-basis of macro-economics is an important area which requires a better understanding of firms' behaviour. In the prediction of variables where the actions of firms are crucially decisive – employment, prices, productivity and the effects of changes in taxation, for example – the traditional generalised theory of the archetypal firm is too blunt an instrument for the fineness of diagnosis that is needed nowadays.

Our concern with firms does not end with a need for better

macro-predictions, nor with an interest in solving the problems involved in reaching the firms' objectives. We are also interested in controlling and encouraging firms to forward the aims of society as a whole. The part played by industry in the pollution problem and in using up the world's scarce resources is now an issue of major public concern. So too is the way in which firms tend to crowd into particular areas of the economy, causing congestion and leaving some regions with unacceptably high levels of unemployment.

There is further the problem that must follow the increasing concentration of the output of most industrial products in the hands of a few large producers – the problem of monopoly. With the development of automation and the sophistication of mass-production techniques, and with the freer international movement of capital investment, all the signs are that the trend towards supranational giants dominating world industry will accelerate.

Pollution, conservation of resources, regional unemployment and monopoly are just four examples of areas in which fuller comprehension of the way firms behave is a prerequisite of any success today in social engineering. The 'invisible hand' that Adam Smith observed, guiding the pursuers of self-interest towards the 'most agreeable' results for society as a whole, did a better job when they numbered in competitive thousands than now when they sit in single figures around the table of a multinational cartel. In fact the guiding hand is apt to be not merely invisible but absent, unless it is supplied by deliberate intervention in the forms of taxation, subsidies and controls. And it is precisely at this point that an accurate knowledge of firms' responses is indispensable. No further justification is needed for a continuing study of the theory of the firm.

References

[1] A. Smith, *An Inquiry into the Nature and Causes of the Wealth of Nations* (1776), ed. E. Cannan (Methuen, London, 1961).

[2] J.-B. Say, *A Treatise on Political Economy* (1803), trans. C. R. Prinsep (Wells & Lilly, Boston, 1821).

[3] J. S. Mill, *Principles of Political Economy* (1848), ed. W. J. Ashley (Longmans, Green, London, 1926).

[4] J. Bentham, *An Introduction to the Principles of Morals and Legislation* (1780) (Hafner, New York, 1948).

[5] C. Menger, *Principles of Economics* (1871), trans. and ed. J. Dingwall and B. F. Hoselitz (Free Press, Glencoe, Ill., 1950).

[6] W. S. Jevons, *The Theory of Political Economy* (1871), 4th ed. (Macmillan, London, 1924).

[7] A. Marshall, *Principles of Economics* (1890), ed. C. W. Guillebaud (Macmillan, London, 1961).

[8] A. Cournot, *Researches in the Mathematical Principles of the Theory of Wealth* (1838), trans. N. T. Bacon (Macmillan, New York, 1972).

[9] L. Walras, *Elements of Pure Economics* (1874), trans. W. Jaffe (Allen & Unwin, London, 1954).

[10] P. Sraffa, 'The Laws of Returns under Competitive Conditions', *Economic Journal* (Dec 1926).

[11] J. Robinson, *The Economics of Imperfect Competition* (Macmillan, London, 1933).

[12] E. H. Chamberlin, *The Theory of Monopolistic Competition* (Harvard U.P., Cambridge, Mass., 1933).

[13] G. L. S. Shackle, *The Years of High Theory* (Cambridge U.P., 1967).

[14] J. B. Hendry, 'The Bituminous Coal Industry', in W. Adams (ed.), *The Structure of American Industry* (Macmillan, New York, 1961).

[15] L. G. Reynolds, 'Competition in the Cotton Textile Industry: A Case Study', in W. Adams and L. B. Traywich (eds.), *Readings in Economics* (Macmillan, New York, 1948).

[16] G. Akerman, 'The Cobweb Theorem: A Reconsideration', *Quarterly Journal of Economics* (Feb 1957).

[17] M. Ezekiel, 'The Cobweb Theorem', *Quarterly Journal of Economics* (1938).

[18] J. A. Schumpeter, *Capitalism, Socialism and Democracy* (Harper & Row, New York, 1942).

[19] J. M. Clark, 'Toward a Concept of Workable Competition', *American Economic Review* (June 1940).

[20] J. M. Clark, *Competition as a Dynamic Process* (Brookings Institution, Washington, D.C., 1961).

[21] S. Sosnick, 'A Critique of Concepts of Workable Competition', *Quarterly Journal of Economics* (Aug 1958).

[22] G. J. Stigler, 'Perfect Competition Historically Contemplated', *Journal of Political Economy* (Feb 1957).

[23] J. de V. Graaff, *Theoretical Welfare Economics* (Cambridge U.P., 1967).

[24] I. M. D. Little, *A Critique of Welfare Economics* (Oxford U.P., 1963).

[25] G. J. Stigler, *Five Lectures on Economic Problems* (Longmans, Green, London, 1949).

[26] R. Triffin, *Monopolistic Competition and General Equilibrium Theory* (Harvard U.P., Cambridge, Mass., 1940).

[27] R. L. Bishop, 'Elasticities, Cross-Elasticities and Market Relationships', *American Economic Review* (1952).

[28] R. L. Bishop, replies to refs. [29]–[31], *American Economic Review* (1953, 1955).

[29] E. H. Chamberlin, 'Elasticities, Cross-Elasticities and Market Relationships: Comment', *American Economic Review* (1953).

[30] W. Fellner, same title as [29], *American Economic Review* (1953).

[31] R. Heiser, same title as [29], *American Economic Review* (1955).

[32] J. S. Bain, 'Chamberlin's Impact on Microeconomic Theory', in [43] and in H. Townsend (ed.), *Price Theory* (Penguin Books, Harmondsworth, 1971).

[33] A. Nicols, 'The Rehabilitation of Pure Competition', *Quarterly Journal of Economics* (1947).

[34] J. S. Bain, *Pricing, Distribution and Employment*, rev. ed. (Holt, Rinehart & Winston, New York, 1953).

[35] G. C. Archibald, 'Chamberlin versus Chicago', *Review of Economic Studies* (Oct 1961).

[36] R. E. Kuenne (ed.), *Monopolistic Competition Theory: Studies in Impact. Essays in Honor of Edward H. Chamberlin* (Wiley, New York, 1966).

[37] L. G. Telser, 'Monopolistic Competition: Any Impact Yet?', *Journal of Political Economy* (Mar–Apr 1968).

[38] H. von Stackelberg, *The Theory of the Market Economy*, trans. A. T. Peacock (William Hodge & Co., London, 1952).

[39] W. J. Baumol, *Economic Theory and Operations Analysis*, 3rd ed. (Prentice Hall, Englewood Cliffs, N.J., 1972).

[40] J. Hadar, *Elementary Theory of Economic Behaviour* (Addison-Wesley, Reading, Mass., 1966).

[41] I. Horowitz, *Decision Making and the Theory of the Firm* (Holt, Rinehart & Winston, New York, 1970).

[42] M. R. Colberg, D. R. Forbush and G. R. Whittaker, *Business Economics: Principles and Cases*, 3rd ed. (Irwin, Homewood, Ill., 1964).

[43] A. D. A. Kaplan, J. B. Dirlam and R. F. Lanzillotti, *Pricing in Big Business: A Case Approach* (Brookings Institution, Washington, D.C., 1958).

[44] D. A. Worcester, 'Why Dominant Firms Decline', *Journal of Political Economy* (Aug 1957).

[45] J. W. Markham, *Competition in the Rayon Industry* (Harvard U.P., Cambridge, Mass., 1952).

[46] C. H. Hession, 'The Metal Container Industry', in W. Adams (ed.), *The Structure of American Industry* (Macmillan, New York, 1961).

[47]   G. J. Stigler, 'The Dominant Firm and the Inverted Umbrella', *Journal of Law and Economics* (Oct 1965).

[48]   G. J. Stigler, 'The Kinky Oligopoly Demand Curve and Rigid Prices', *Journal of Political Economy* (Oct 1947).

[49]   J. W. Markham, 'The Nature and Significance of Price Leadership', *American Economic Review* (Dec 1951).

[50]   R. B. Tennant, 'The Cigarette Industry', in W. Adams (ed.), *The Structure of American Industry* (Macmillan, New York, 1961).

[51]   J. S. Bain, 'Price Leaders, Barometers and Kinks', *Journal of Business* (July 1960).

[52]   R. F. Lanzillotti, 'Competitive Price Leadership: A Critique of Price Leadership Models', *Review of Economics and Statistics* (Feb 1957).

[53]   A. Oxenfeldt, 'Professor Markham on Price Leadership', *American Economic Review* (June 1952).

[54]   W. Fellner, *Competition among the Few* (Knopf, New York, 1949).

[55]   G. J. Stigler, 'A Theory of Oligopoly', *Journal of Political Economy* (Feb 1964).

[56]   R. L. Hall and C. J. Hitch, 'Price Theory and Business Behaviour', *Oxford Economic Papers* (May 1939).

[57]   P. M. Sweezy, 'Demand under Conditions of Oligopoly', *Journal of Political Economy* (Aug 1939).

[58]   J. L. Simon, 'A Further Test of the Kinky Oligopoly Demand Curve', *American Economic Review* (Dec 1969).

[59]   P. Pashigian, 'Conscious Parallelism and the Kinky Oligopoly Demand Curve', *American Economic Review, Papers and Proceedings* (May 1967).

[60]   C. J. Hawkins, 'An Exploration of the Kinked Demand Curve Hypothesis', Southampton University Discussion Papers in Economics and Econometrics, No. 7102 (1971).

[61]   R. F. Harrod, 'Theory of Imperfect Competition Revised', in his *Economic Essays* (Macmillan, London, 1952).

[62] P. W. S. Andrews, *Manufacturing Business* (Macmillan, London, 1949).

[63] H. R. Edwards, 'Price Formation in Manufacturing Industry and Excess Capacity', *Oxford Economic Papers* (Feb 1965).

[64] H. R. Edwards, *Competition and Monopoly in the British Soap Industry* (Oxford U.P., 1962).

[65] J. S. Bain, 'A Note on Pricing in Monopoly and Oligopoly', *American Economic Review* (Mar 1949).

[66] J. S. Bain, *Barriers to New Competition* (Harvard U.P., Cambridge, Mass., 1956).

[67] P. Sylos-Labini, *Oligopoly and Technical Progress* (Harvard U.P., Cambridge, Mass., 1962).

[68] F. Modigliani, 'New Developments on the Oligopoly Front', *Journal of Political Economy* (Aug 1964).

[69] D. K. Osborne, 'The Role of Entry in Oligopoly Theory', *Journal of Political Economy* (Aug 1964).

[70] M. Mann *et al.*, 'Comment: Entry and Oligopoly Theory', *Journal of Political Economy* (Aug 1965).

[71] D. W. Gaskins, 'Optimal Dynamic Limit Pricing', presented to North American Regional Conference New York, 1969, and abstracted in *Econometrica* (July 1970).

[72] P. Pashigian, 'Limit Price and the Market Share of the Leading Firm', *Journal of Industrial Economics* (July 1968).

[73] M. I. Kamien and N. L. Schwartz, 'Limit Pricing and Uncertain Entry', *Econometrica* (May 1971).

[74] M. I. Kamien and N. L. Schwartz, 'Uncertain Entry and Excess Capacity', *American Economic Review* (Dec 1972).

[75] O. E. Williamson, 'Selling Expense as a Barrier to Entry', *Quarterly Journal of Economics* (1963).

[76] J. N. Bhagwati, 'Oligopoly Theory, Entry Prevention and Growth', *Oxford Economic Papers* (Nov 1970).

[77] J. S. Bain, 'Economies of Scale, Concentration, and the Condition of Entry in Twenty Manufacturing Industries', *American Economic Review* (Mar 1954), reprinted in J. S. Bain, *Essays on Price Theory and Industrial Organisation* (Little, Brown, Boston, 1972), which also

contains [65] and much of Bain's other work on the entry-forestalling model.

[78] H. M. Mann, 'Seller Concentration, Barriers to Entry and Rates of Return in Thirty Industries, 1950–1960', *Review of Economics and Statistics* (Aug 1966).

[79] J. T. Wenders, 'Entry and Monopoly Pricing', *Journal of Political Economy* (Oct 1967).

[80] W. S. Comanor and T. A. Wilson, 'Advertising, Market Structure and Performance', *Review of Economics and Statistics* (Nov 1967).

[81] P. J. D. Wiles, *Price, Cost and Output* (Basil Blackwell, Oxford, 1961).

[82] J. Johnston, *Statistical Cost Analysis* (McGraw-Hill, New York, 1960).

[83] C. F. Pratten, *Economies of Scale in Manufacturing Industry*, University of Cambridge, Department of Applied Economics, Occasional Paper No. 28 (Cambridge U.P., 1971).

[84] C. F. Pratten, R. M. Dean and A. Silberston, *The Economies of Large-Scale Production in British Industry*, University of Cambridge, Department of Applied Economics, Occasional Paper No. 3 (Cambridge U.P., 1965).

[85] National Bureau of Economic Research, *Cost Behaviour and Price Policy* (New York, 1963).

[86] National Bureau of Economic Research, *Business Concentration and Price Policy* (Princeton U.P., 1955).

[87] C. A. Smith, 'Survey of Empirical Evidence on Economies of Scale,' in [86] and abridged in G. C. Archibald (ed.), *The Theory of the Firm* (Penguin Books, Harmondsworth, 1971).

[88] M. Friedman, 'Comment', from [86].

[89] A. Silbertson, 'Economies of Scale in Theory and Practice', *Economic Journal* (Mar 1972) supplement.

[90] M. A. Utton, *Industrial Concentration* (Penguin Books, Harmondsworth, 1970).

[91] N. Kaldor, 'The Irrelevance of Equilibrium Economics', *Economic Journal* (Dec 1972).

[92]   O. E. Williamson, 'Economics as an Antitrust Defense', *American Economic Review* (Mar 1968).

[93]   C. K. Rowley, *Antitrust and Economic Efficiency*, Macmillan Studies in Economics (Macmillan, London, 1973).

[94]   H. Leibenstein, 'Allocative Efficiency vs. "X-Efficiency"', *American Economic Review* (June 1966).

[95]   O. E. Williamson, 'Managerial Discretion and Business Behaviour', *American Economic Review* (Dec 1963).

[96]   R. Caves *et al.*, *Britain's Economic Prospects* (Brookings Institution, Washington, D.C., 1968).

[97]   J. M. Clark, 'Competition: Static Models and Dynamic Aspects', *American Economic Review* (May 1955).

[98]   S. G. Winter and E. S. Phelps, 'Optimal Price Policy under Atomistic Competition', in E. S. Phelps (ed.), *Microeconomic Foundations of Employment and Inflation Theory* (Norton, New York, 1970).

[99]   R. J. Ball, *Inflation and the Theory of Money* (Allen & Unwin, London, 1964).

[100]   E. T. Penrose, *The Theory of the Growth of the Firm* (Basil Blackwell, Oxford, 1959).

[101]   J. Robinson, 'Imperfect Competition Revisited', *Economic Journal* (Sept 1953).

[102]   G. B. Richardson, *Information and Investment* (Oxford U.P., 1960).

[103]   G. L. S. Shackle, *Expectation, Enterprise and Profit: The Theory of the Firm* (Allen & Unwin, London, 1970).

[104]   F. Machlup, 'Marginal Analysis and Empirical Research', *American Economic Review* (Sept 1946).

[105]   F. Machlup, 'Theories of the Firm: Marginalist, Behavioural, Managerial', *American Economic Review* (Mar 1967).

[106]   R. Thierauf and R. Grosse, *Decision Making through Operations Research* (Wiley, New York, 1970).

[107]   R. Schlaifer, *Analysis of Decisions under Uncertainty* (McGraw-Hill, New York, 1969).

[108]   E. S. Mills, *Price, Output and Inventory Policy* (Wiley, New York, 1962).

[109] M. D. Steuer and A. P. Budd, 'Price and Output Decisions of Firms: A Critique of E. S. Mills' Theory', *Manchester School of Economic and Social Studies* (Mar 1968).

[110] J. von Neumann and O. Morgenstern, *The Theory of Games and Economic Behaviour* (Princeton U.P., 1944).

[111] R. D. Luce and H. Raiffa, *Games and Decisions* (Wiley, New York, 1957).

[112] L. E. Fouraker and S. Siegel, *Bargaining Behaviour* (McGraw-Hill, New York, 1963).

[113] J. W. Friedman, 'An Experimental Study of Co-operative Duopoly', *Econometrica* (July–Oct 1967).

[114] W. J. Baumol, 'Models of Economic Competition', in P. Langhoff (ed.), *Models, Measurement and Marketing* (Prentice-Hall, Englewood Cliffs, N.J., 1965) and in H. Townsend (ed.), *Price Theory* (Penguin Books, Harmondsworth, 1972).

[115] M. Shubik, 'The Uses of Game Theory in Management Science', *Management Science* (1955), reprinted in B. V. Carsberg and H. C. Edey (eds.), *Modern Financial Management* (Penguin Books, Harmondsworth, 1969).

[116] A. A. Alchian, 'Uncertainty, Evolution and Economic Theory', *Journal of Political Economy* (June 1950).

[117] S. G. Winter, 'Economic "Natural Selection" and the Theory of the Firm', *Yale Economic Essays* (spring 1964).

[118] A. A. Alchian and H. Demsetz, 'Production, Information Costs, and Economic Organisation', *American Economic Review* (Dec 1972).

[119] A. A. Berle and G. Means, *The Modern Corporation and Private Property* (Macmillan, New York, 1932).

[120] R. A. Gordon, *Business Leadership in the Large Corporation* (California U.P., Berkeley, 1961).

[121] R. J. Larner, 'Ownership and Control in the 200 Largest Nonfinancial Corporations: 1929 and 1963', *American Economic Review* (Sept 1966).

[122] R. J. Monsen, J. S. Chiu and D. E. Cooley, 'The Effect of Separation of Ownership and Control on the

Performance of the Large Firm', *Quarterly Journal of Economics* (Aug 1968).

[123] J. P. Shelton, 'Allocative Efficiency vs. X-Efficiency: Comment', *American Economic Review* (Dec 1967).

[124] A. Papandreou, 'Some Basic Problems in the Theory of the Firm', in B. F. Haley (ed.), *A Survey of Contemporary Economics*, vol. II (Irwin, Homewood, Ill., 1952).

[125] T. Scitovsky, 'A Note on Profit Maximisation and its Implications', *Review of Economic Studies* (1943), reprinted in American Economic Association, *Readings in Price Theory* (Allen & Unwin, London, 1953).

[126] O. E. Williamson, 'Managerial Discretion and Business Behaviour', *American Economic Review* (Dec 1963).

[127] O. E. Williamson, 'A Model of Rational Managerial Behaviour', in [152].

[128] O. E. Williamson, *The Economics of Discretionary Behaviour* (Prentice-Hall, Englewood Cliffs, N.J., 1964).

[129] O. E. Williamson, *Corporate Control and Business Behaviour* (Prentice-Hall, Englewood Cliffs, N.J., 1970).

[130] D. R. Roberts, *Executive Compensation* (Free Press, Glencoe, Ill., 1959).

[131] J. W. McGuire *et al.*, 'Executive Incomes, Sales and Profits', *American Economic Review* (Sep 1962).

[132] W. J. Baumol, 'On the Theory of Oligopoly', *Economica* (1958).

[133] W. J. Baumol, *Business Behaviour, Value and Growth* (Macmillan, New York, 1959).

[134] W. G. Shepherd, 'On Sales Maximising and Oligopoly Behaviour', *Economica* (1962).

[135] C. J. Hawkins, 'On the Sales Revenue Maximisation Hypothesis', *Journal of Industrial Economics* (Apr 1970).

[136] C. J. Hawkins, 'The Revenue Maximisation Oligopoly Model: Comment', *American Economic Review* (June 1970).

[137] R. Rosenberg, 'Profit Constrained Revenue Maximisation: Note', *American Economic Review* (Mar 1971).

[138] M. H. Peston, 'On the Sales Maximisation Hypothesis', *Economica* (May 1959).

[139] M. Hall, 'Sales Revenue Maximisation: An Empirical Examination', *Journal of Industrial Economics* (Apr 1967).

[140] L. Waverman, 'Comment' on [139], *Journal of Industrial Economics* (Nov 1968).

[141] B. D. Mabry and D. L. Siders, 'An Empirical Test of the Sales Maximisation Hypothesis', *Southern Economic Journal* (Jan 1967).

[142] E. Ames, *Soviet Economic Processes* (Irwin, Homewood, Ill., 1965); reprinted in G. C. Archibald (ed.), *The Theory of the Firm* (Penguin Books, Harmondsworth, 1971).

[143] M. J. Kafoglis, 'Output of the Restrained Firm', *American Economic Review* (Sep 1969).

[144] H. Averch and L. L. Johnson, 'Behaviour of the Firm under Regulatory Constraint', *American Economic Review* (Dec 1962).

[145] J. L. Stein and G. H. Borts, 'Behaviour of the Firm under Regulatory Constraint', *American Economic Review* (Dec 1972).

[146] H. A. Simon, 'Theories of Decision Making in Economics and Behavioural Science', *American Economic Review* (1959); reprinted in G. P. E. Clarkson (ed.), *Managerial Economics* (Penguin Books, Harmondsworth, 1968).

[147] H. A. Simon, 'On the Concept of Organisational Goal', *Administrative Science Quarterly* (June 1964); reprinted in H. I. Ansoff (ed.), *Business Strategy* (Penguin Books, Harmondsworth, 1969).

[148] H. A. Simon, 'A Behavioural Model of Rational Choice', *Quarterly Journal of Economics* (Feb 1955).

[149] H. A. Simon, *Models of Man* (Wiley, New York, 1957).

[150] R. M. Cyert and J. G. March, *A Behavioural Theory of the Firm* (Prentice-Hall, Englewood Cliffs, N.J., 1963).

[151] W. J. Baumol and M. Stewart, 'On the Behavioural Theory of the Firm', in [166].

[152] K. J. Cohen and R. M. Cyert, *Theory of the Firm: Resource Allocation in a Market Economy* (Prentice-Hall, Englewood Cliffs, N.J., 1965).

[153] R. M. Cyert and M. I. Kamien, 'Behavioural Rules and the Theory of the Firm', in A. Phillips and O. E. Williamson (eds.), *Prices: Issues in Theory, Practice, and Public Policy* (Pennsylvania U.P., Philadelphia, 1967).

[154] R. J. Monsen and A. Downs, 'A Theory of Large Managerial Firms', *Journal of Political Economy* (June 1965).

[155] J. Margolis, 'The Analysis of the Firm: Rationalism, Conventionalism and Behaviourism', *Journal of Business* (July 1958).

[156] G. C. Archibald (ed.), *The Theory of the Firm* (Penguin Books, Harmondsworth, 1971).

[157] G. P. E. Clarkson, 'Interactions of Economic Theory and Operations Research', in A. R. Oxenfeldt (ed.), *Models of Markets* (Columbia U.P., New York, 1963), and in G. P. E. Clarkson (ed.), *Managerial Economics* (Penguin Books, Harmondsworth, 1968).

[158] R. B. Heflebower, 'Full Costs, Cost Changes and Prices', in [86].

[159] J. Markham, review of [43] in *American Economic Review* (June 1959).

[160] B. Fog, *Industrial Pricing Policies*, trans. I. E. Bailey (North-Holland Publishing Co., Amsterdam, 1960).

[161] R. F. Lanzillotti, 'Pricing Objectives in Large Companies', *American Economic Review* (Dec 1958) and 'Pricing Objectives in Large Companies: Reply', *American Economic Review* (Sep 1959).

[162] W. W. Haynes, 'Pricing Practices in Small Firms', *Southern Economic Journal* (Apr 1964).

[163] I. F. Pearce, 'A Study in Price Policy', *Economica* (1956).

[164] U.S. Senate Committee on the Judiciary Report, *Administered Prices: Automobiles* (Washington, D.C., 1958).

[165] R. Marris, *The Economic Theory of 'Managerial' Capitalism* (Macmillan, London, 1964).

[166] R. Marris and A. Wood (eds.), *The Corporate Economy* (Macmillan, London, 1971).

[167]   W. J. Baumol, 'On the Theory of Expansion of the Firm', *American Economic Review* (Dec 1962).

[168]   J. H. Williamson, 'Profit, Growth and Sales Maximisation', *Economica* (Feb 1966).

[169]   D. A. Kuehn, 'Stock Market Valuation and Acquisitions: An Empirical Test of One Component of Managerial Utility', *Journal of Industrial Economics* (Apr 1961).

[170]   A. Singh and G. Whittington, *Growth, Profitability and Valuation* (Cambridge U.P., 1968).